BIBLE MEMORY FOR BEGINNERS

---

5 PRACTICAL, SIMPLE STEPS ON HOW TO MEMORIZE THE BIBLE SCRIPTURE VERSES, CHAPTERS, AND ENTIRE BOOKS

O. A. JOSEPH

CONTENTS

Introduction   ix

SECTION ONE

1. BENEFIT—KNOWING GOD MORE
   INTIMATELY   3
   A Call   4
   God Is a Rewarder   5

2. NO TIME? THREE WAYS TO FIND TIME TO
   MEMORIZE SCRIPTURE   7

3. BENEFIT—BECOMING MORE LIKE JESUS   11
   Beholding and Becoming   12

4. STEP 1—BIBLE MEMORY STARTS ON OUR
   KNEES   14
   Take Action: Five Prayers for FREED Scripture
   Memory   16

SECTION TWO

5. BENEFIT—EFFECTIVE PRAYER   21
   Praying the Bible   22

6. BAD MEMORY? TOO OLD? SAYS WHO?   25
   Memory Lapses   25
   Lifestyle Impact   26
   You Too Can Memorize Scripture!   27

7. BENEFIT— DEEPER BIBLE STUDY   28
   Digging Deeper   28
   Fuel for Deep Meditation   29

8. STEP 2— HOW TO CHOOSE WHAT BIBLE
   VERSES OR PASSAGES TO MEMORIZE   32
   Verses, Chapters, or Books?   32
   Bite-Size Snacks   33
   A Generous Portion   34

Which Verse or Passage?   35
Which Bible Translation Should You Use?   38
Take Action   39

9. SOME VERSES AND PASSAGES YOU
SHOULD KNOW   40
Christ-Centered   40
Other Gems   42

SECTION THREE

10. WHAT TYPE OF LEARNER ARE YOU?   47
How Memory Works   47
Identifying Your Learning Style   49
Experimenting With Each Technique.   51

11. BENEFIT—ENJOY GREATER VICTORY OVER
SIN AND TEMPTATION   52
Understanding Temptation: A Biblical
Perspective   52
The Sword of the Spirit   53

12. TOO HARD? TRY THIS!   56

13. STEP 3— PREPARE   60
Eating an Elephant   60
Index Cards   61
Paper and Pen   62
Familiarity Principle   63

14. PRACTICE—VISUAL   64
Color It   64
Picture It   65
Post It! Stick It!   66
Mirror It   67
The Glue Method For Memorizing Bible
References   68

SECTION FOUR

15. BENEFIT— LED MORE BY THE HOLY SPIRIT   73

16. STEP 4— MEMORIZE   76
How Many Verses Per Day?   78
Word-Perfect   79

17. PRACTICE—VERBAL   81
Don't Whisper!   81
Inflect and Accentuate   82
Pray It   82
Sing It   83

18. PRACTICE— AUDIAL   85
Shadow It   85
Shadow Yourself   86
While Asleep   87

19. PRACTICE— SPATIAL   88
Use It or Lose It!   88
Walk It In   90
Move It Out   90
Give Me a Break!   91
The Buddy System   92

20. PRACTICE—WRITTEN   94
CatchWords and CatchPhrases   94
Pattern It Out   96
Rewrite It   97
Embrace Multilingual Approach   98

21. BENEFIT—BE A POWERFUL WITNESS   100
Sharing Your Personal Testimony vs. the Gospel   101

SECTION FIVE

22. STEP 5— HOW TO NEVER FORGET WHAT
YOU MEMORIZED   107
Spaced Review   108

23. BENEFIT—WORDS SEASONED WITH SALT   110
    For Mutual Edification   110
    Helping Others with Biblical Wisdom   111

24. IS BIBLE MEMORIZATION ESSENTIAL OR
    OPTIONAL?   114

25. WHAT TO DO WHEN YOU WANT TO GIVE UP!   118
    Pray!   120
    Your Big Whys   121
    Reach Out   122

    Final Request   123

    References   125

INTRODUCTION

I am not a memory expert!

Bible memorization is not something that comes easily to me! I have not won any special memory championships. Like many of you, I am just an everyday Christian with no special abilities—a fellow traveler on the narrow way. I am writing this not because I know any better, but because I have searched and found a way that works. I have taken many turns and stumbled over many different methods in my quest, making me realize that hiding God's Word in our hearts is not as complicated as most of us assume. Memorizing Scripture is actually easier than we think!

Over the last few years of my walk with the Lord, I have learned both by study and experience how to effectively write God's Word on the tablets of my heart so that I can have it as constant nourishment for my inner man and a light for my feet! I have memorized lots of Scripture with the help of the

Holy Spirit, so I am convinced that any Christian can, by His help, learn and recall Bible verses, chapters, entire books, and more!

With a few practical tips, every believer has the ability to store Scripture, word-for-word, in their minds and hearts. With a bit of time and effort, you—yes you!—can successfully memorize God's Word and have one of the most rewarding experiences of your life. There's nothing as remarkable as an encouraging Bible verse springing forth from your memory with the help of the Holy Spirit when you need to hear it the most. One thing is sure: You'll never regret having spent time memorizing God's Word.

The question we need to ask is not whether we can memorize verses or not, but whether we want to! Ask yourself:

- Are you hungry to know God more deeply?
- Do you desire to become more like Christ and grow in character?
- Do you yearn to be continually led and guided by the Holy Spirit?
- Do you want your prayers to be effective and receive answers?
- Would you like to experience daily triumph over temptation, sin, Satan, and the flesh?
- Do you desire to become a more effective soul winner, witnessing with confidence for Jesus?
- Do you long to be more spiritually fit to go through the hard times of life as well as more equipped to meet the needs and opportunities you face each day?

If you answered yes to any of these questions, then welcome to the enriching and life-changing journey of hiding God's Word in your heart, and having it as a constant source of strength and nourishment for your spirit, soul, and body.

How to Use This Book

This book is designed to be thought-provoking and intensely practical. You will find a straightforward, simple, proven Scripture memory method that will help you know and hide God's Word in your heart.

Apart from the easy-to-use, five-step Scripture memory method, there are also lots of tried-and-true techniques that will propel your ability to learn and remember Bible verses like you never thought possible. You will undoubtedly find at least one or more that is the right approach for you. So, refrain from boxing yourself into any single idea of tackling memory tasks. The important thing is not that you follow the concepts like a recipe but that you take my suggestions and experience and adapt them to your situation. Whether you need help starting or improving your Scripture memory endeavor, put the ideas here to work and find what is best for you. As you do, you will be able to figure out those that fit you, your learning style, personality, etc. Then fine-tune them and stick to them.

A combination of these ideas is likely to provide the best results, as recreating an exact method might not be the best way for you to recollect something. Also, incorporating a variety of these techniques into the way you memorize Bible verses should help keep the journey from becoming boring and mere routine. Who said memorizing Scripture can't be fun?

This book will not only equip you with many proven and effective Scripture memorization techniques but will also motivate you to treasure God's Word in your heart, thereby eliminating the typical excuses.

If you are like most of us, you are always busy every day with family, church, work, and other things constantly demanding your attention. We all could use more time, but I unfortunately cannot add even one more second to your day. However, applying the ideas in this book will help you make the best use of your time to memorize Scripture and know God more intimately during your many daily activities. You should not postpone a closer walk with God until you have more time. You need Him today. Your need to memorize Scripture today cannot be overemphasized.

My burning desire and prayer are that, as you use this book to embark on this soul-searching, life-altering, and rewarding journey, your relationship with God will grow richer and more profound than you ever thought it would. This path will help enable you to be daily transformed into the image of his Son, Jesus Christ, with ever-increasing glory, which comes from the Lord, who is the Spirit (2 Cor. 3:18).

The man who has the Bible and the Holy Spirit in his heart has everything which is absolutely necessary to make him spiritually wise. He needs no priest to break the bread of life for him. He needs no ancient traditions, no writings of the Fathers, and no voice of the Church, to guide him into all truth. He has the well of truth open before him, and what more can he want? Yes! though he be shut up alone in a prison or cast on a desert island—though he never sees a church or minister again—if he only has the Bible, he has got the infallible guide and needs no other. If he only has the will to read that Bible properly, it will certainly teach him the road that leads to heaven. It is here alone that infallibility resides. It is not in the Church. It is not in the Councils. It is not in ministers. It is only in the written Word.

J. C. Ryle

SECTION ONE

1

BENEFIT—KNOWING GOD MORE INTIMATELY

I keep asking that the God of our Lord Jesus Christ, the glorious Father, may give you the Spirit of wisdom and revelation, so that you may know him better.
Ephesians 1:17

According to Hebrews 8:11, there is a sense in which every Christian—from the least to the greatest—has come to know the Lord. Our relationship with Him starts once we become His children through faith in Christ Jesus alone for the forgiveness of our sins. "For to all who did receive him, to those who believed in his name, he gave the right to become children of God—children born not of natural descent, nor of human decision or a husband's will, but born of God" (John 1:13 NIV).

However, there is another sense in which our knowledge of God needs to deepen beyond the point of our initial salvation and adoption into His family. The Apostle Paul, despite his years of walking with the Lord, expressed in Philippians 3:8-14 that he had not yet attained to knowing Christ as he ought, but he was pressing on toward that goal. If this was the case for Paul, how much more does it apply to us? Every sincere believer can resonate with this aspiration, as the desire to know God more profoundly is a universal longing among those born of God by the power of the Holy Spirit. It is a deep longing within our hearts to understand better who God is and deepen our relationship with Him.

A Call

As Christians, we are called to continuously grow, particularly in our knowledge of the Holy One. This calling and principle is explicitly stated in 2 Peter 3:17-18: "You therefore, beloved, knowing this beforehand, take care that you are not carried away with the error of lawless people and lose your own stability. But grow in the grace and knowledge of our Lord and Savior Jesus Christ. To him be the glory both now and to the day of eternity. Amen."

Was this not also Paul's prayer for the Ephesians, as expressed in Ephesians 1:17: "I keep asking that the God of our Lord Jesus Christ, the glorious Father, may give you the Spirit of wisdom and revelation, so that you may know him better"?

We must avoid reaching a point where we are entirely satisfied with our knowledge of Christ. There is always more. He is the wellspring of living water that never runs dry. Charles Spurgeon aptly expressed this truth: "He who does not long to know more of Christ knows nothing of Him yet. Whoever has sipped this wine will thirst for more, for although Christ satisfies, it is such a satisfaction that the appetite is not saturated, but stimulated" (Alcorn, 2010). Therefore, let us wholeheartedly immerse ourselves in the pursuit of knowing God more deeply.

To press on in knowing the Lord, we must begin by considering the most effective way He has chosen to reveal His nature, personality, character, and works to us. Instead of relying on preconceived thoughts about God, let us commune and fellowship with Him by memorizing and meditating on His attributes and excellencies as revealed in His written Word. The act of hiding Scriptures in our hearts serves as a means to genuinely comprehend God as He is, fostering a closer walk with Him. The more we acquaint ourselves with Him, the stronger the desire to deepen that knowledge becomes. Just as love deepens with knowledge, the deeper our understanding of God, the more genuine our love and reverence for Him, whether in times of unspeakable joy or great trials and distress.

God Is a Rewarder

God possesses a remarkable way of concealing His glories within the pages of Scripture, inviting us to actively search them out. Proverbs 25:2 beautifully captures this concept: "It is the glory of God to conceal things, but the glory of kings is to search them out." This verse emphasizes the divine mystery woven into God's Word and highlights the honor bestowed upon those who earnestly seek, explore, and unravel the profound truths concealed within its sacred pages.

While I may initially read a verse or passage and comprehend its meaning in context, it is my experience that, often through subsequent readings, committing it to memory, and meditating upon it, the Scripture unexpectedly unveils facets of God's character and works that I somehow missed before. Indeed, His Word is an ever-expanding treasure trove that yields more beautiful gems of insights the deeper we dig into its profound depths.

An old godly man once said, "So often, God will not show His face to those who are content to read over verses once or twice but only to those who dig, those who desire, and those who show some perseverance and effort." The question remains: Will you set your heart today to be counted among those who diligently seek the profound truths hidden within the pages of God's Word?

Many of us desire to draw closer to God, but this requires time to read and memorize Scripture. While we drag from one day to another, some may struggle to find that time, as other things distract them from seeking God's divine presence. They complain that there are never enough hours in a day, but we can manage our days in ways that allow us to dedicate time to God. In the following chapter, let's explore some strategies to navigate this challenge.

2

NO TIME? THREE WAYS TO FIND TIME
TO MEMORIZE SCRIPTURE

*Look carefully then how you walk, not as unwise but as wise, making
the best use of the time, because the days are evil. Therefore do not be
foolish, but understand what the will of the Lord is.*
Ephesians 5:15-17

But someone may well say, "I don't have enough time
right now to memorize Scripture!"

The perception that you lack sufficient time can be a significant challenge when you want to memorize the Bible.
However, if we are sincere with ourselves and speak the
honest truth, we will realize that the problem is not with the
time: the problem is with us. In reality, the excuse of busy-
ness holds very little weight, considering we find time for

other activities we want to do, like watching TV, spending time with family, or browsing our phones.

According to 1 Corinthians 9:25, "Every athlete exercises self-control in all things. They do it to receive a perishable wreath, but we an imperishable." It all comes down to your priorities: to the value you place on the Word of God and your spiritual health. An athlete organizes his life around his training because it is crucial if he is to achieve his goals, so he puts in the extra effort required to see that he works hard daily while still meeting his other obligations. Memorizing Scripture must take a high priority in your life if you truly desire to grow spiritually.

Now here are some practical tips to help you find the time needed for you to memorize Scripture:

1. **Make a Time Adjustment:** Deeply reflect on how you spend your time. In Ephesians 5:15-17, Paul the Apostle makes it clear that God's will for us is to be wise in making the best use of time because the days are evil. Take this seriously, pray about it, and evaluate your schedule. Set aside some activities you enjoy but are unnecessary in light of eternity. If you cannot find the time to feed on the Scriptures every day, then you are busier than God intended you to be in the first place. If you want your relationship with the Lord to thrive, you must adjust your priorities.

2. **Make Use of "Waiting Time":** If you are currently in a season with tight schedules, I recommend using those small blocks of time that occur naturally between activities. These are the "waiting" moments when you are not really doing

anything and can easily be used to memorize and review Scripture.

Here are some examples:

- waiting for the bus/metro/train to arrive
- waiting while going to work/school or home
- waiting to pay at the supermarket
- waiting in a traffic jam in your car
- waiting for the coffee you ordered
- waiting for the water to boil
- waiting for the arrival of a friend for a scheduled meeting
- waiting in lifts or elevators
- waiting for something to load or download on your computer
- waiting for someone to answer the door after you knock, etc.

These brief moments of your day pass by unused and, over time, add up to a significant amount of lost time. Of course, you can't avoid these waiting situations; they are natural parts of your day. However, you can make good use of them to hide God's Word in your heart. Put a verse on the back of your phone and, instead of opening social media, turn your phone over and study the verse. We will discuss many methods to make better use of this time.

3. **"Kill Two Birds With One Stone"**: Or, in other words, aim to make the most of your time by doubling its use. If you're similar to most people, there are likely several instances

during the day when you are occupied with routine tasks that don't require your complete focus—moments when your hands are occupied, but your mind is free. Take advantage of these chunks of time to review and memorize Scripture.

For example, let's take a closer look at everyday household chores. Tasks such as dusting, sweeping, vacuuming, washing dishes, feeding pets, folding laundry, changing bedding, mopping floors, watering plants, mowing the lawn, weeding the garden, taking out the trash, washing the car, and more are part of our daily routines that keep us occupied without requiring significant mental effort. So, why not train yourself to put into practice some of the Scripture memory ideas you will learn in this book and turn these routine tasks into opportunities to hide God's Word in your heart?

3

BENEFIT—BECOMING MORE LIKE JESUS

And we all, with unveiled face, beholding the glory of the Lord, are being transformed into the same image from one degree of glory to another. For this comes from the Lord who is the Spirit.
2 Corinthians 3:18

We frequently hear sermons, read books, and sing songs about becoming more and more like Jesus. Nobody who professes to be a Christian would deny wanting to conform more to the image of Christ! And we know and believe that when He shall appear, we shall be like Him because we shall see Him as He is. But often, on this side of eternity, it is easy to become discouraged when we look at ourselves. We wonder if we will ever get to that place where we are more holy and more like the image of Jesus than ourselves.

According to Romans 8:29, God's purpose in creating and redeeming us is to have a family of children conformed to the image of His Son. From the outset, His plan has been to shape you into the likeness of Christ. His desire is for Christ to be formed in you. This is not just your destiny; it's a profound privilege. However, the question arises: How does this transformation change occur in us, and how can we actively experience this profound metamorphosis?

Beholding and Becoming

The answer lies in the renewal of our minds, which occurs as we look to Jesus and set our thoughts on Him as revealed in the Bible. A mind that is being transformed and renewed is one saturated with and controlled by the Word of God. Christlikeness will only become a reality in our lives if we steadily savor Jesus. We must see, behold, and gaze on his beauty found in the pages of Scripture. This process is beautifully encapsulated in 2 Corinthians 3:18 (NIV): "And we all, who with unveiled faces contemplate the Lord's glory, are being transformed into his image with ever-increasing glory, which comes from the Lord, who is the Spirit."

With the help of the Holy Spirit, Bible memorization is one of the things that has this effect—it makes our gaze on Jesus steadier and clearer. It helps us focus on Christ, to love and to enjoy Him in all his person: intellectually, emotionally, spiritually, and aesthetically by admiring Him in his beauty.

This should be one of the ongoing cries of our hearts: "Lord, make me more like You!" To daily grow into the image of Jesus is our goal, and it should remain so until the day we go to be with Him. But, we often fall so short. If we had to measure ourselves, we would see just how far apart from His likeness we are! It can be discouraging if we keep our eyes on our weaknesses and shortcomings. But, in order to be changed into his likeness with ever-increasing splendor, we must keep looking at Christ and contemplating his glory.

If you run to Scripture, and you stop there, then you've missed the entire point of Scripture. The point of Scripture is to send you on to Christ in a correct fashion, that you might feed from Him.
–Paul Washer

Keep your soul fit to manifest the life of the Son of God. Never live on memories; let the Word of God be always living and active in you.
–Oswald Chambers

4

STEP 1—BIBLE MEMORY STARTS ON OUR KNEES

But in everything by prayer and supplication with thanksgiving let your requests be made known to God.
Philippians 4:6

Praying is not usually the first thing that comes to mind when seeking methods or techniques for anything. Often, we desire special tricks and tips to unlock hidden strategies that will catapult us forward. However, as Christians, prayer is the most apparent key God has given us to open any door. Therefore, asking for God's help and wisdom should be our first step in any venture, especially when it deals with His own Word.

While you may be enthusiastic about delving straight into the Bible and focusing on honing your memorization skills, it's important to remember that the primary objective isn't to memorize the Scriptures as quickly and extensively as possible. It's not akin to a final exam that you have to cram for. The essence of Scripture memorization lies in developing a more profound knowledge of God. Consequently, as you embark on this deep and life-altering journey of internalizing God's Word, it is crucial to seek Him in prayer diligently. God must be an integral part of this endeavor because we are engaging with His Word—His divinely inspired written Word to us.

In Philippians 4:6, Paul encourages the believers in the Philippian church to pray in every situation. This instruction holds true for our everyday lives, implying that we should depend on God for and in everything, including the memorization of the Holy Scriptures. Bible memory without prayer is barren and unfruitful. Therefore, it is vital for us to be not only people rooted in God's Word but also individuals devoted to prayer. Ensure that your pursuit of Scripture memorization is saturated with prayers.

James 1:5, in the larger context of the entire Bible, also emphasizes the importance of seeking wisdom from God when we lack it. Whether it pertains to significant, life-altering decisions, such as the trials and persecution the believers faced in the early church as they read the letter from James, or even more minor matters in our day, like choosing which passage of Scripture to memorize, God doesn't automatically grant wisdom without our active participation. Instead, He expects us to ask for it. This implies the necessity of prayer.

Prayer is the foundational and most crucial step in memorizing God's Word. Bible memory must start on our knees. Prayer establishes the groundwork for Scripture memorization to become a spiritual exercise of treasuring God's Word in our hearts rather than merely a hobby or a skill we are striving to master. Through prayer, we express our reliance on the Holy Spirit, seek divine assistance, acknowledge our need for wisdom, and actively pursue God's guidance. This approach aligns with God's inclination to assist, guide, and reveal His truths to those who earnestly seek Him.

Take Action: Five Prayers for FREED Scripture Memory

1. **Focus:** Pray that God would grant you a focused, disciplined mind to be more diligent in memorizing the Bible. Ask Him to help you develop this godly habit that will feed your soul for life (Gal. 5:22).

2. **Renewal:** Pray that God would make you a doer of the Word. Ask Him to inform and renew your mind with His Word, directing your daily life. Request that the seeds from Scripture grow mightily, producing more tangible and noticeable fruit in your practical living (James 1:22, Matt. 7:24).

3. **Enlightenment:** Pray that God would illuminate your mind and enlighten the eyes of your heart. Ask Him to open your spiritual eyes to wondrous things and glimpses of glory you cannot see by yourself in the Word. Ask God to enlighten your understanding, to quicken your devotion, and to warm your affections (Eph. 1:17–18, Psalm 119:18).

4. **Enjoying Jesus:** The most critical aspect of Scripture memory and the great goal of feeding on God's Word through memorization is knowing and enjoying Jesus. Ask God for the Holy Spirit to keep your eyes focused on Jesus so that you might behold, gaze, and enjoy His glory and the beauty of His excellence. Pray for help in grasping how each verse or passage you memorize relates to the person and work of Jesus (John 17:3, John 5:39, Luke 24:27).

5. **Daily Desire:** Pray that God would help you desire and treasure the words of His mouth more than your necessary daily food. Seek His intervention to ignite a renewed hunger and thirst in your heart: a profound love, interest, and longing for His Word. You will come to recognize its surpassing value over gold and its sweetness exceeding that of honey in a honeycomb. Pray that the practice of Scripture memory doesn't become a lifeless routine but rather a source of joy, all for the glory of Christ (Job 23:12, Psalm 19:10).

SECTION TWO

5

BENEFIT—EFFECTIVE PRAYER

If you remain in Me, and My words remain in you,
ask whatever you wish, and it will be done for you.
John 15:7 (NASB)

We have all experienced moments when we set aside time to pray, but we struggle to find the right words. It's not a lack of willingness—sometimes our minds just seem to go blank. If you have ever encountered such a situation, remember that it doesn't mean that you are less of a Christian. Even the most devout Christians encounter times when they can't find the right words to pray, despite their sincere intentions.

One effective solution to this issue of stunted prayer time is to memorize and pray the Scriptures. Thomas Brooks emphasized that the surest way to safeguard your prayers and ensure their effectiveness is to have one eye on God's laws and the other on His promises (Brooks, 2013). Utilizing God's own words from Scripture and pleading His promises at the throne of grace will infuse your prayers with tremendous power and bolster your confidence. As stated in John 15:7, "If you remain in Me, and My words remain in you, ask whatever you wish, and it will be done for you." Throughout history, those who have excelled in prayer have consistently been diligent students of the Word of God.

Furthermore, effective prayer is inspired and directed by the Holy Spirit. Hence, the Scripture in Ephesians 6:18 directs us to pray in the Spirit on all occasions and with all kinds of prayers and requests. But how do we pray in the Spirit? To pray in the Spirit simply means to pray in alignment with the Word of God, which has been divinely inspired by the Holy Spirit.

Lastly, Jesus in His Sermon on the Mount instructed us to pray for God's will to be done. But how can we pray for God's will if we do not know it? To pray effectively, it is essential to actively search the Scriptures and familiarize ourselves with God's revealed will. By immersing ourselves in His Word and hiding it in our hearts, we become equipped to pray more fervently and in accordance with His will, thereby leading to more answers to our prayers.

Praying the Bible

John Piper was asked about using the Scriptures as a base to form our prayers, and instead of arguing over formats and spontaneity, he encourages it. Why? He says that it stops us from useless repetitions and only concentrating on our own problems, and rather helps us focus on who God is and what He wants. In addition, many Bible passages are actual prayers, so to model ours on those examples is an excellent way to learn. Nevertheless, he does caution against simply repeating what is written as this will be meaningless—"We are praying meaning. We are not just praying words" (2017).

As a practical help, Piper goes on to explain how we can do this (2017):

> The Scriptures either tell us something about God and Christ when we are reading so that we can praise him. Or, they tell us something about what God and Christ and the Holy Spirit have done so that we can thank him and express faith in it. Or, they tell us what God expects from us so that we can cry out for his help. Or, they tell us about something we failed to do so that we can confess our sins. So, it seems to me that virtually all of the Bible is doing one or more of those four things: something about God, something about what he has done, something about what he expects, something about how we have failed, so that they naturally lead into praise to God, thanks to God, crying for help to God, and confession of sin to God.

Prayer is nothing but the promise reversed, or God's Word formed into an argument, and retorted by faith upon God again... Furnish yourself with arguments from the promises to enforce your prayers and make them prevalent with God. The promises are the ground of faith, and faith, when strengthened will make you fervent, and such fervency

speeds and returns with victory out of the field of prayer… The mightier anyone is in the Word, the mightier he will be in prayer.
–William Gurnall

6

BAD MEMORY? TOO OLD? SAYS WHO?

Memory Lapses

Memory lapses are a common occurrence for many of us. From forgetting where we placed our car keys to struggling to recall someone's name after meeting them, these lapses are a universal experience regardless of age, gender, or profession. However, it's crucial to recognize that unless you have been clinically diagnosed with brain problems, having occasional memory lapses doesn't equate to having a poor memory overall. This misconception is often heard, especially as individuals age.

Many people mistakenly believe that their academic performance or lack thereof directly correlates with their ability to memorize Scripture. However, one's performance in school doesn't necessarily reflect their memory capacity outside of an academic setting.

Others claim to be too elderly and that their memory must have shrunk or degenerated. While aging may impact cognitive function to some extent, it doesn't necessarily mean that memory capabilities diminish entirely. Our bodies may show signs of slowing down and getting tired more quickly, yet we might not be cognitively impaired. Studies have shown that individuals can maintain cognitive function at a high level well into their older years (Riddle, 2007).

The truth is, you have a much better memory than you think. The issue often lies not in our memory capacity but in our willingness to exert effort and our lack of adequate practice methods. Many claim they can't memorize anything, yet they can effortlessly recall song lyrics from decades ago or recite detailed sports statistics of their favorite players. This demonstrates that memory capabilities are often underestimated and that we tend to remember what is personally significant to us.

Lifestyle Impact

In practical terms, there are various ways to enhance memory, and they do not necessarily have to do with our brains but instead with our bodies as a whole. For example, a Harvard study revealed that our daily diet is one factor that will determine whether our memory is working at its best or not. The study showed that those who ate more saturated fats performed worse on memory tests than those who ate healthy diets (Brody, 2022). In addition, regular exercise and adequate sleep also positively affect our brains. These lifestyle factors play a significant role in optimizing cognitive function and memory retention. Therefore, taking care of our overall health is crucial for supporting optimal brain function.

You Too Can Memorize Scripture!

It's essential to reject the notion that a poor memory or age is a barrier to memorizing Scripture. With determination and the help of the Holy Spirit, believers in Christ of any age can learn the art of memorizing Scripture. Our memory is a muscle that can be strengthened through Christ, who empowers us through His Spirit. You already have a fantastic memory to start hiding God's Word. With a little effort and commitment, you'll be amazed at what you can commit to memory by following the simple strategies in this book. Yes, you too can memorize Scripture!

7

BENEFIT— DEEPER BIBLE STUDY

Study to shew thyself approved unto God, a workman that needeth
not to be ashamed, rightly dividing the word of truth.
2 Timothy 2:15 (KJV)

Digging Deeper

As believers in Christ Jesus, we recognize the significance of studying the Bible, but there are indeed seasons and moments when it can feel less enjoyable and more of a drag! Have you ever experienced your Bible study time becoming more laborious? Maybe you find yourself grappling with finding the right passages and cross-references related to the text you're studying? Wouldn't it be truly beneficial if, during your study, you could recall other relevant verses, enabling you to compare Scripture with Scripture, gaining insights as you read precept upon precept and line upon line?

Memorizing Scripture makes it possible for the Scripture you are studying to be spontaneously cross-indexed and enriched with other passages hidden in your heart. The promise of the Holy Spirit, as stated in John 14:26, assures us that He will be our Helper, guiding us in understanding and recalling all that Jesus has taught. As the Holy Spirit works in us, these cross-referenced passages are brought to our remembrance, facilitating a more accurate interpretation of the Scriptures in context. It's only when we have interpreted a biblical passage correctly that we can then effectively apply its teachings to our lives, bringing honor and glory to God through our actions and faith.

> Now I am no prophet, nor the son of a prophet, but one thing I can predict; that every one of our new converts that goes to studying his Bible, and loves this book above every other book, is sure to hold out. The world will have no charm for him; he will get the world under his feet, because in this book he will find something better than the world can give him. (D. L. Moody)

Fuel for Deep Meditation

This Book of the Law shall not depart from your mouth, but you shall meditate on it day and night, so that you may be careful to do according to all that is written in it. For then you will make your way prosperous, and then you will have good success. –Joshua 1:8

Scripture clearly teaches that one of the signs we belong to God is that we delight in His Word and meditate on it day and night (Heb 10:16; Psalm 119:97, 148).

But how can we meditate on God's Word day and night if it isn't available, right there in our minds? Once you've memorized Scriptures, you can use the fleeting moments between activities or quiet hours of the night to dwell on God's Word. One of the most notable benefits of memorizing Scripture is that it stimulates meditation. It supplies the necessary fuel for deep contemplation. And through meditation, the Scripture permeates the very fabric of our souls, infusing it with strength, making the Word truly active and impactful to our inner beings.

When you have committed a verse or passage of Scripture to memory, you can then meditate on it at any moment throughout the day or night, allowing you to experience the blessings of biblical meditation as beautifully depicted in Psalm 1:1-3:

"Blessed is the man who walks not in the counsel of the wicked, nor stands in the way of sinners, nor sits in the seat of scoffers; but his delight is in the law of the Lord, and on his law he meditates day and night. He is like a tree planted by streams of water that yields its fruit in its season, and its leaf does not wither. In all that he does, he prospers."

Thomas Watson reminds us that simply reading the Bible is not enough to warm our hearts towards spiritual things. He writes, "The reason our affections are so chill and cold in spiritual things is because we do not warm ourselves more at the fire of meditation" (2012). Biblical meditation goes beyond just reading the words on the page; it involves pondering on God's Word and allowing the verse or passage time to reveal its meaning and work in us. It's like "chewing on the cud," taking time to fully understand and absorb the words, rather than simply swallowing them.

Remember that it is not hasty reading—but serious meditation on holy and heavenly truths, which makes them prove sweet and profitable to the soul. It is not the mere touching of the flower by the bee which gathers honey—but her abiding for a time on the flower which draws out the sweet. It is not he who reads most, but he who meditates most—who will prove to be the choicest, sweetest, wisest, and strongest Christian!
–Thomas Brooks

8

STEP 2— HOW TO CHOOSE WHAT BIBLE VERSES OR PASSAGES TO MEMORIZE

Verses, Chapters, or Books?

Whether you're tackling entire books, chapters, or key verses, Bible memorization is always a valuable investment of time. As 2 Timothy 3:16 reminds us, "All Scripture is breathed out by God and profitable for teaching, for reproof, for correction, and for training in righteousness." You'll never regret dedicating extended time to memorizing God's Word.

But where do you start? Do you focus on individual verses, immerse yourself in a rich passage, or attempt to memorize an entire book of the Bible? When is the right time to take the plunge into more challenging material?

Just like a runner doesn't attempt a marathon without training, starting with smaller portions and gradually building up your capacity is essential. This approach helps train your mind in areas that may have lain dormant for some time. Trying to tackle too much too soon can lead to discouragement and burnout.

So, start with bite-size verses in a context that you can easily grasp and retain. As you become more comfortable with memorization, you'll naturally find yourself eager to expand your repertoire and tackle more extensive passages.

Bite-Size Snacks

This method of memorizing a series of short passages, verses, or key sections within their context, provides a broad knowledge of essential truths, making it ideal and valuable for new believers seeking a comprehensive range of Scripture on various topics or those beginning their journey of Scripture memorization.

When selecting short sections or verses for memorization, it's crucial that you understand the context and choose complete thoughts. Whether it's a single verse or a grouping of two or four verses that constitute an entire thought, it's vital to avoid using God's Word out of context.

If you search the internet for the top verses to memorize, you'll likely come across a list of commonly cited verses, many of which align with those provided in the upcoming chapter. As a beginner, it's advisable to stick with these well-known verses and avoid obscure passages, as they may be more challenging to understand or apply effectively.

A Generous Portion

Once you've mastered several verses and are ready to tackle a new challenge, consider setting your sights on larger portions of Scripture. This second method is primarily geared, though not exclusively, toward those who have been consistently memorizing Scripture for some time and have experienced success in doing so.

As you develop the habit of memorization and grow comfortable with it, tackling chapters or even entire books can be a deeply rewarding experience. Similar to consuming a full meal, having whole chapters hidden in your heart provides spiritual sustenance over extended periods, nourishing and strengthening your inner being. While individual verses are beneficial, they can be likened to snacks—you may need to replenish more frequently to keep going. In contrast, memorizing entire chapters or books allows for a more substantial and enduring source of spiritual nourishment.

The benefits of memorizing entire books of the Bible are indeed remarkable:

1. **No Scripture Is Wasted:** Memorizing the entire book ensures that no verses are overlooked or skipped. Often, we tend to focus only on the verses we like, but when you remember the entire book, there are no leftovers.

2. **Capturing the Tone:** Memorizing the entire book allows you to grasp the heart and tone of the writer much more effectively than focusing on individual verses.

3. **Understanding the Flow of the Argument:** Particularly in Paul's letters, he builds his arguments progressively. By knowing the entire book, you can follow his train of thought and logical progression.

4. **Appreciating Context:** Understanding the context is crucial, as one verse out of context can convey a different meaning. Memorizing the entire book helps you grasp the context and appreciate the verses in their intended entirety. For example, Philippians 4:13 "For I can do everything through Christ, who gives me strength," is often quoted without considering the context provided by the surrounding verses. In this verse, Paul is explaining that because he has experienced hardships, he knows God will stay with him through future challenges. It is a message of encouragement through hardship, not merely a mantra of confidence.

5. **Efficiency and Ease:** Learning logically and systematically by memorizing entire books is more efficient and easier compared to memorizing scattered phrases from different contexts. Being able to link verses together as a whole allows memorization to come more naturally because it facilitates comprehension and retention.

Which Verse or Passage?

Which verse or passage should you choose? While 2 Timothy 3:16-17 emphasizes the overall significance of all Scripture being inspired by God for teaching, reproof, correction, and training in righteousness. It's important to note that randomly opening the Bible and learning the first text you see may not be an effective method.

A Bible Scripture passage relevant to what you may be going through will be easier to memorize than one that speaks about a topic that is foreign to you. All of us are better at remembering things that are significant or essential to us. When something is of particular interest to us, it is easier to learn and remember. Therefore, as a beginner, make it a point to memorize verses and passages you intend to use that are significant to you.

Search and memorize those verses that:

- God has used to minister to you in the past and would be helpful in your personal walk with Christ and your ministry to others. Perhaps there was a verse that was meaningful in your own journey to trust God in a particular situation. Or maybe a spiritual role model helped you by sharing with you a verse when you were struggling.
- Meet specific needs in your life. Memorize for your soul! We are not into mechanical memorizing. Instead, make sure you remember verses that will help your soul in the fight of faith, especially those that help you in the areas you are currently struggling. These will include verses that encourage you about God's love and grace and verses that warn you about how that specific behavior and sin displease God. Memorizing relevant Scriptures to overcome a particular sin you struggle with is an excellent means of enjoying your victory in Christ

Jesus. For example, if you are struggling with bitterness, memorize the Scriptures about how much God has forgiven you and the importance of forgiveness. This way, the next time you are tempted to be bitter or resentful, those Scriptures will provide you with greater power to resist temptation and encourage you to forgive.

Here are four ways to find key verses and passages about any area or topic you wish to memorize:

1. My favorite and highly recommended way is to read through the entire Bible, looking out for passages on topics that are currently important to you. As you read through and understand the context of the verse, make and keep a list in your journal containing Scriptures that touch you significantly or draw your attention. Write them down in your list. And, if you wish, write down the date and briefly describe when, where, and why this verse(s) caught your attention.

2. Get a textbook on theology and look up the topic you are interested in learning. In a good book like *Systematic Theology: An Introduction to Biblical Doctrine* by Wayne Grudem, each section will have many Scriptures to support its teachings.

3. Use a topical Bible such as *Nave's Topical Bible* or *Torrey's Topical Textbook*. These books have huge lists, sorting many great Scriptures into thousands of different topics and categories. Both are in the public domain, which means you can get a digital copy for free.

4. Use a Bible concordance such as the *Strong's Expanded Exhaustive Concordance of the Bible* and look up particular words relating to your interest and their corresponding verses.

Which Bible Translation Should You Use?

There are so many translations and versions to choose from, and it is basically up to you which one you choose. However, there are a few things to take into account.

1. Select a version written in a way you can understand—not too archaic or difficult to digest. This is essential because our minds quickly absorb things we understand. Though a paraphrased version of the Bible like *The Living Bible, Good News Bible,* and *The Message* are easy to understand and also good for devotional reading, I would suggest that you memorize from a "true" translation of your choice and not from a paraphrased version because those are more prone to error and misinterpretation. In contrast, a "true" translation is likely to represent the original biblical text closely and will not make as many interpretations and applications of the Bible's teaching for you.

2. Prayerfully research the major translations' strengths and weaknesses in order to make a wise choice. This is most important because some versions have strange interpretations of passages that could be misleading. Go for one that is widely accepted and used in sound biblical churches.

3. Once you have chosen your preferred translation and
    started memorizing from a particular version, stick
    with it as much as possible because every version has
    its own way of presentation that you will get used to
    over time. As a beginner, trying to memorize from
    more than one Bible version will only work to
    confuse you.

Take Action

Implementing the practical suggestions from this chapter,
prayerfully select a Bible verse or verses you desire to hide in
your heart. In Step 3 and subsequent chapters, I will offer
guidance on how to prepare your selected text and provide
you with diverse practical techniques to facilitate smoother
and more effective memorization.

9

SOME VERSES AND PASSAGES YOU SHOULD KNOW

Christ-Centered

If you're still unsure about where to start or which verse to begin with, here are some Christ-centered verses and passages to help you get started on your journey. As you continue reading the Bible, keep an eye out for more verses that resonate with you and add them to your Bible memory list.

Verses

1. Isaiah 9:6: *"For to us a child is born, to us a son is given; and the government shall be upon his shoulder, and his name shall be called Wonderful Counselor, Mighty God, Everlasting Father, Prince of Peace."*
2. Mark 10:45: *"The Son of Man came not to be served but to serve, and to give his life as a ransom for many."*

3. John 3:16: *"For God so loved the world, that he gave his only Son, that whoever believes in him should not perish but have eternal life."*

4. Romans 5:8: *"God shows his love for us in that while we were still sinners, Christ died for us."*

5. Romans 6:23: *"The wages of sin is death, but the free gift of God is eternal life in Christ Jesus our Lord."*

6. Romans 8:1: *"There is therefore now no condemnation for those who are in Christ Jesus."*

7. Romans 8:32: *"He who did not spare his own Son but gave him up for us all, how will he not also with him graciously give us all things?"*

8. 2 Corinthians 5:21: *"For our sake he made him to be sin who knew no sin, so that in him we might become the righteousness of God."*

9. 2 Corinthians 8:9: *"You know the grace of our Lord Jesus Christ, that though he was rich, yet for your sake he became poor, so that you by his poverty might become rich."*

10. 1 Timothy 1:15: *"The saying is trustworthy and deserving of full acceptance, that Christ Je-sus came into the world to save sinners, of whom I am the foremost."*

11. 1 John 4:10: *"In this is love, not that we have loved God but that he loved us and sent his Son to be the propitiation for our sins."*

12. Revelation 5:9: *"Worthy are you to take the scroll and to open its seals, for you were slain, and by your blood you ransomed people for God from every tribe and language and people and nation."*

Passages

1. Isaiah 53:4–6
2. Romans 3:23–24
3. Romans 4:4–5
4. 1 Corinthians 15:3–4
5. Galatians 3:13–14
6. Ephesians 2:4–5
7. Philippians 2:6–8
8. Colossians 1:19–20
9. Colossians 2:13–14
10. Titus 3:4–7
11. Hebrews 2:14–17
12. 1 Peter 2:22–25

Other Gems

There are so many other key verses and passages that can be learned to encourage, teach, and remind us of God's work in our lives. Here are a few of them:

Verses

1. Psalm 55:22: *"Cast your burden upon the LORD and He will sustain you; He will never let the righteous be shaken."*
2. Psalm 119:11: *"I have stored up your word in my heart, that I might not sin against you."*
3. Proverbs 3:5: *"Trust in the LORD with all your heart, and do not lean on your own understanding."*
4. Jeremiah 29:11: *"For I know the plans I have for you, declares the LORD, plans for welfare and not for evil, to give you a future and a hope."*

5. Matthew 6:33: *"But seek first the kingdom of God and his righteousness, and all these things will be added to you."*
6. Romans 8:28: *"But seek first the kingdom of God and his righteousness, and all these things will be added to you."*
7. Hebrews 11:1: *"Now faith is the assurance of things hoped for, the conviction of things not seen."*
8. 1 John 1:9: *"If we confess our sins, he is faithful and just to forgive us our sins and to cleanse us from all unrighteousness."*
9. 2 Timothy 1:7: *"For God gave us a spirit not of fear but of power and love and self-control."*

Passages

1. Psalm 23:1-6
2. Matthew 28:18-20
3. Ephesians 5:18-21
4. Philippians 4:4-7
5. Colossians 3:15-17
6. James 1:2-5

SECTION THREE

10

WHAT TYPE OF LEARNER ARE YOU?

He causes us to remember his wonderful works.
Psalm 111:4 (NLT)

How Memory Works

Despite extensive research and numerous studies exploring its physical structure and sophisticated functions, the brain remains one of the most intricate and least understood organs in our body. Comparable to a super-computer's capacity to store vast amounts of information—trillions of bytes of data—our utilization of this incredible organ is often confined to routine activities, such as recalling bank account details and performing daily tasks.

To understand the workings of the mind and how memory functions, it is best to simplify it into terms we can under-stand. The brain can be compartmentalized into four main sections that each perform different tasks ranging from balance to touch, sight, and memory. Two of these areas serve as memory functions: the frontal lobe and the temporal lobe. The frontal lobe is where short-term memories are stored along with other information that is deemed not critical. These thoughts or data are only kept for very short spurts; on average, this lobe holds only about seven memories at a time (Harvard University, 2011). On the other hand, any ideas, events, and information that are filed and kept for an extended period of time are fixed into what is known as the temporal lobe, and these become long-term.

There are three main stages for anything to become a memory.

1. **Encoding:** This is when information is received and understood. It is taken into the brain and processed in a way that can be stored: visually (how it looks), acoustically (how it sounds), semantically (what it means), and in a tactile manner (how it feels). At this point, the information is still transient and has not been locked in as a memory, only filtered so that the mind can assess what kind of data it is (Harvard, 2011).

2. **Storage:** This next part determines whether the information will go to short-term or long-term memory. Everything is processed through the short-term memory first, and only certain items are then passed on to be kept for extended periods in the long-term memory. Often, rehearsal and repetition

are factors that ensure that memories are filed into the temporal lobe for safekeeping (Harvard, 2011).

3. **Retrieval:** This is actually the most important! We mistakenly think that memory is how much you can amass, but that is useless if you cannot get to it when you need to. This is the stage where you find out whether you can actually recall any of the stored information or not. Short-term memories are remembered sequentially, while long-term data is by association (Harvard, 2011).

Although it might seem like nothing goes into your brain or that you cannot remember much, Wilder Penfield revealed through experiments that the brain retains anything with conscious effort (Sletten, n.d.). That means whatever we want to remember takes some work on our part, through which it is committed to our brains for storage.

Identifying Your Learning Style

As individuals, we are all blessed with diverse gifts from God that may differ from those bestowed upon others (Rom. 12:6-8, 1 Peter 4:10-11). Additionally, our personalities vary greatly, as God has designed us uniquely. Consequently, our methods of learning, interacting, and retaining information are greatly influenced by our individuality and who we are as individuals.

Knowing how memory functions is one thing, but understanding how you as a person can best receive, store, and retrieve information is the key. Each of us is unique, and our learning methods are influenced by our distinct personalities, styles, and cognitive processes. Discovering these nuances empowers you to identify techniques that align with your individuality, enabling you to retain and recall Bible verses and passages optimally.

Looking at a broader scale, many agree that there are seven learning styles, but these can easily be grouped into the four main areas I mentioned above. In 1987, Neil Fleming introduced the VARK method that he had designed to assess an individual's learning preferences (Broadbent, 2021). As we explore these styles, it is beneficial to evaluate which learning style resonates most with you.

- **Visual:** Pictures are essential to these people. They love graphs, displays, and anything that can be seen with their eyes rather than writing and reading. Color-coded notes and doodles fill your Bible.
- **Aural/Audial:** Anything that can be heard is locked in. Conversations, lectures, and even music are easy for these learners to absorb as long as there is not an overload of sounds. Audible Bibles are a winner in this category! Mnemonic devices work for these people.
- **Read/Write:** Notes and more notes fill these people's books and Bibles. Reading and summarizing is their favorite way of soaking up information. Highlighting key points or verses and making lists are ways that they make associations. Anything that can be read and written is in their wheelhouse.

- **Spatial/Kinesthetic:** These are the tactile learners that need to touch and feel. Short bursts of studying are best for them as long as movement is involved. Anything practical suits this group, and they learn better while on the go, working with a study partner, or using flash cards.

Experimenting With Each Technique.

This book contains several helpful techniques for memorizing Bible verses and passages, recognizing that not every method will align with your personal learning style. While some strategies may seem like a waste of time, frustrating, or ineffective to you, the diversity of approaches ensures that there are likely one or two—or perhaps even more—that will seamlessly integrate with your unique way of learning. It's important not to dismiss any technique outright based on initial impressions. Even if a method doesn't immediately seem to complement your learning preferences, giving it a try is worthwhile. Experimenting with each technique is the only way to truly discover what works best for you. This openness to exploration can lead to finding effective strategies for memorization that you might not have initially considered.

11

BENEFIT—ENJOY GREATER VICTORY OVER SIN AND TEMPTATION

Thy word have I hid in mine heart, that I might not sin against thee.
Psalm 119:11 (KJV)

Understanding Temptation: A Biblical Perspective

Temptation is a topic that many shy away from discussing, yet it remains an integral aspect of everyday life, posing a considerable challenge for Christians around the world. The epistle of James in verses 1:13-15 offers vital insights into the nature of temptation, clarifying a crucial point: being tempted is not a sin. It's a common aspect of the fallen human condition to be enticed and carried away by our own lust or personal desires. The critical juncture occurs when these desires or lust have conceived and matured; this is when lust gives birth to sin. Once sin has fully developed, it results in death. This progression from temptation to sin, and ultimately to its grave consequence, underscores the importance of vigilance and resistance at the initial stage of temptation to prevent sin's gestation and eventual fatal outcomes.

The Sword of the Spirit

During His earthly ministry, Jesus faced temptation but remained sinless, standing firm on the solid foundation of God's Word. The account in Matthew 4 provides a profound example of how to resist temptation and cause Satan to flee, as we see in the confrontation between good and evil played out in the wilderness. Jesus was tempted by the devil three times, and each time, He countered with Scripture He had memorized, wielding the sword of the Spirit: the Word of God. If there was a more effective method to combat temptation, Jesus would surely have used it. His reliance on Scripture proves that it is the most potent approach for overcoming the lures of Satan, the world, and our own desires.

Reflecting more on Jesus' temptation as described in Luke 4:13, it's clear that Satan often looks for opportune moments to tempt us to sin. In such critical times, we might not have immediate access to a Bible. And, even if we do, it's of little use if we're not familiar with relevant verses or passages. But with a substantial reservoir of God's Word stored in our hearts, the Holy Spirit can swiftly bring to our remembrance the appropriate Scriptures we need. A timely piece of scriptural truth, prompted by the Holy Spirit, can become a powerful weapon that makes a significant difference in a spiritual battle against Satan's lies.

The young men referenced in 1 John 2:13-14 were strong and overcame the evil one precisely because the Word of God dwelled within them. As we face the lure of sin, it is solely through Christ-revealing Scripture, brought to our awareness by the Holy Spirit, that will help us overcome the temptation because of the superior value of Christ over sin's fleeting pleasures. This principle is reinforced in Psalm 119:11, which teaches that the more Scripture we hide in our hearts, the better prepared we become to withstand the schemes of the devil and avoid sinning against God. With the aid of the Holy Spirit, committing Scripture to memory fortifies us to withstand temptation and enjoy a life of victory in Christ.

J. C. Ryle sees the Bible as a weapon to fight against the devil's schemes, but it needs to be in our hearts, not gathering dust on the bookshelf (2018):

> The Word is the sword of the Spirit. We shall never fight a good fight if we do not use it as our principal weapon. The Word is the lamp for our feet. We shall never keep the king's highway to heaven if we do not journey by its light. It is not sufficient to have the Book. We must actually read it, and pray over it ourselves. It will do us no good if it only lies still in our houses. We must be actually familiar with its contents and have its texts stored in our memories and minds. Knowledge of the Bible never comes by intuition. It can only be obtained by diligent, regular, daily, attentive, wakeful reading.

The Word of God will be to you a bulwark and a high tower, a castle of defense against the foe. Oh, see to it that the Word of God is in you, in your very soul, permeating your thoughts, and so operating upon your outward life, that all may know you to be a true Bible-Christian, for they perceive it in your words and deeds.
–Charles Spurgeon

12

TOO HARD? TRY THIS!

But by the grace of God I am what I am, and his grace toward me was not in vain. On the contrary, I worked harder than any of them, though it was not I, but the grace of God that is with me.
1 Corinthians 15:10

Indeed, everything seems hard before it becomes easy! Nothing truly worthwhile is going to be easy. If something is attained without any effort, it's likely it won't last very long. Lasting results are achieved through dedication, effort, and time spent focusing on the goal. Whether it's training for a sports event, studying for exams, or changing your diet, these challenges may seem insurmountable at first, like towering mountains with no clear path to the summit. However, each journey begins with a single step, followed by another, and gradually, you find your rhythm. With the passage of time and some discipline, the process becomes easier and more natural, evolving into a lifestyle.

In a similar vein, memorizing Scripture is worth the effort; it is a wise investment of time and energy that offers returns immensely more valuable than the initial deposit. Therefore, do not give up.

Consider a work scenario: If you have a target to meet at work, and you are meant to memorize some lines for the presentation that have refused to stick, would you give up knowing that your job depends on how well you are able to deliver? Why, then, do we give up so easily when it comes to memorizing the Scriptures? The vigor of our spiritual life will be in exact proportion to the place held by the Bible in our lives and thoughts.

Scripture memorization is a discipline that strengthens with practice. Your spiritual "fitness" improves with consistent effort, just as physical exercise holds value, as noted in 1 Timothy 4:8, which suggests that "bodily training is of some value." The more you engage in memorizing Scripture, the more skilled you become. In fact, this practice not only enhances your ability to retain and recall Scriptural passages but also improves your memory in other areas of life.

The University of North Carolina concurs with this viewpoint, advocating that perseverance in the initial stages of memorization leads to improved retention of facts and texts, making the process more intuitive over time. They note, "Some of these techniques can feel strange at first or take some time to develop. The more you practice them, the easier and more natural they become, and the more information you can commit to memory" (UNC, 2018).

However, training the brain and enhancing memory is not a one-time endeavor; it requires ongoing effort, much like maintaining physical fitness through sports. Ceasing practice can lead to noticeable declines. It is, indeed, a lifestyle commitment. Once you embrace this approach and witness its benefits, you'll realize that the discipline and hard work are well worth the effort. As Harvard Health points out, "Building and preserving brain connections is an ongoing process, so make lifelong learning a priority" (Harvard Health, 2020).

And here's the good news: you are not alone in this journey. If we relied solely on our own strength, we might give up at the first sign of difficulty. However, Philippians 4:13 offers us a powerful reminder: "I can do all things through Christ who gives me strength." While Paul was primarily speaking of his ability to be content in every situation through Christ's strength, for all Believers, this principle of reliance on Christ's strength holds true universally, including in the discipline of Bible Memorization. Do you believe you can do all things through Christ, who strengthens you by His Spirit in your inner being? Does this belief extend to memorizing Scripture? Since you are capable, by the grace of God working in you, will you take action? Why not start today?

If the thought of establishing an effective memory routine seems daunting, remember that it's perfectly okay to start small. Simply choose one verse to begin with. There are numerous straightforward, efficient tips and tools available that have aided many in this journey, myself included, and have yielded tangible results. Explore these techniques, tailor them to fit your needs, and embark on a new lifestyle. I pray that these insights will be a blessing to you!

I want to know one thing, the way to heaven; how to land safely on that happy shore. God Himself has condescended to teach the way; for this end, He came from heaven. He hath written it down in a book. Give me that book! At any price give me the Book of God!
–John Wesley

13

STEP 3— PREPARE

You might feel eager to start memorizing Scripture and simply want to open the Bible and dive in. That enthusiasm is commendable! However, diving in without proper preparation can lead to dwindling enthusiasm, especially when you realize that the verses might only stick in your short-term memory, making recall difficult later on.

As with any training or exercise, preparation is key to ensure you're equipped to handle the task at hand. Rather than merely reading the verse and hoping it sticks, consider ways to prepare it for effective retention and long-term memory storage.

Eating an Elephant

Attempting to memorize an entire verse or chapter at once can feel overwhelming. You might start with plenty of motivation and be excited that you know the first part well, but quickly lose your energy and zone out while memorizing the last few parts. The old adage "The best way to eat an elephant is one bite at a time" offers a metaphorical guide on how to tackle seemingly insurmountable tasks, such as memorizing Scripture.

Whether it's a single verse or an entire chapter you are memorizing, break it down into smaller, more manageable sections for optimal memorization and retention. It is actually easier to retain and remember the Scripture when you work in smaller bits.

Divide the entire section into portions, then further segment these portions into sentences, and finally, break down the sentences into manageable phrases. Ensure that you maintain the natural flow of the language and create divisions that allow for appropriate pauses. This approach facilitates easier encoding and storage of the text in your memory.

Index Cards

Earlier, I discussed two creative ways to find time for memorizing Scripture: capturing small blocks of time that naturally occur between activities and making the most of your available time. One effective method to implement these ideas is to write your chosen verse or passage onto index cards. Carry these cards with you wherever you go, enabling you to memorize and review Scripture on the go. Index cards are readily available online or can be easily made at home, making them a convenient and accessible tool for anyone seeking to commit Scripture to memory.

Paper and Pen

But please DO NOT simply copy, paste, and print your chosen Scriptures on these index cards. Write them out by hand. You may wonder, "What is the point of rewriting everything out by hand?" One of the best ways to memorize faster and retain anything longer is to write it out by hand. That's because writing down something stimulates a part of the brain called the Reticular Activating System, which acts as a sort of filter for everything your brain has to process, giving more value to what you are actively focusing on.

Writing down Scriptures by hand is indeed slower and more cumbersome than printing them out, but it forces your brain to engage in some heavy mental lifting, and these efforts will improve your comprehension and retention in the long run. Conversely, simply printing them out can be done in a fairly mindless fashion, with little analysis or synthesis by the brain.

It might seem old-school, but almost every major center or learning institute agrees that the act of rewriting information, whether it is in color, with pictures, or simply words, is highly effective and a timeless method of memorizing. According to research from the University of North Carolina, "Writing appears to help us more deeply encode information that we're trying to learn because there is a direct connection between our hand and our brain" (2018).

In summary, for better comprehension and long-term retention, I highly recommend that you write them out by hand because the act of writing engages your motor skills and memory, among other things. There's more muscle memory involved, and it requires different types of cognitive processing that can improve Scripture memorization and retention. So, find a way that best suits you, but get out the pen or the colored markers and start writing.

Familiarity Principle

Meaning is vital to memory. A crucial step for Scripture memory is to become familiar with the Scripture you have chosen to memorize. The more you understand the Scripture you are memorizing, the more deeply the words will take root in your heart. Therefore, it is crucial that you read, reread, and comprehend the text in its proper context, allowing you to grasp the big picture and its meaning.

Also, try to look up new words and concepts you need clarified and strive to gain a basic understanding of these terms to the extent that you can explain their meanings to a friend, a five-year-old, or someone who speaks English as a second language. Though some of these new words and concepts may be found in a conventional English dictionary, referring to a reputable Bible dictionary can help obtain accurate and relevant definitions.

And if possible, study the text deeply. This will not only draw out riches from God's Word for your soul but will help engrave them on your heart fairly easily.

In the upcoming chapters, we will explore further techniques to assist you in the memorization process.

14

PRACTICE—VISUAL

Color It

Colors speak louder than words. Who in their right mind doesn't delight in the beauty of colors? They not only brighten our world but can also serve as a powerful tool to enhance your Scripture memorization. By assigning different colors to various phrases, sentences, or paragraphs on your index cards, you create a visual memory aid that enriches your visual experience. This keeps your brain engaged and focused during memorization sessions, strengthening your recall of Scripture.

All you need to do is write the first phrase, sentence, or paragraph in blue, and then the next one in black, the following in green, then in red, and so on.

Just keep interchanging the colors based on your choice. It is your verse, so fill in your colors.

Let's take the passage from Isaiah 53:4-6 (NIV) and apply this line by line.

RED: *Surely he took up our pain and bore our suffering,*

BLACK: *yet we considered him punished by God stricken by him, and afflicted.*

BLUE: *But he was pierced for our transgressions,*

BLACK: *he was crushed for our iniquities;*

RED: *the punishment that brought us peace was on him,*

BLUE: *and by his wounds we are healed.*

BLACK: *We all, like sheep, have gone astray,*

RED: *each of us has turned to our own way;*

BLUE: *and the Lord has laid on him the iniquity of us all. Isaiah fifty-three, verses four to six.*

Picture It

Consider the timeless adage, "A picture is worth a thousand words," which holds considerable truth. Although it may seem minor, sketching or doodling a picture linked to a verse or passage you're trying to memorize can significantly enhance retention. This visual association does help embed the text more deeply in your memory, making it easier to recall over time.

To harness this technique, jot down the Scripture on an index card and embellish the margins with illustrations or doodles that capture the essence of the verse. Your drawing doesn't need to be intricate; even simple drawings can be profoundly effective. Here are a few suggestions to get you started:

- Psalm 1:1—a chair
- Galatians 2:12—a plate with a spoon in it
- Psalm 119:11—a heart with a Bible inside of it
- Luke 8:16—a candlestick
- Matthew 5:13—a saltshaker over planet earth

Post It! Stick It!

As I mentioned earlier, capitalizing on the underutilized moments during everyday household tasks can be a transformative approach to Scripture memorization. These seemingly trivial spans of time, when properly utilized, can significantly enhance your memorization efforts. Sticky notes, a familiar and versatile tool, emerge as an invaluable ally in this endeavor. Their simplicity and accessibility have made them a staple in organizing various aspects of life, from academic studies to household management. Now, let's delve into strategies for employing sticky notes to master Scripture memory effectively:

1. Start by purchasing a pack of Post-It notes and selecting colors that resonate with your personal style. Choosing your favorite colors adds an element of enjoyment and personalization to the memorization process.
2. Write down the verse or passage on a Post-It note. Depending on the length, you might need multiple

notes. Continue until the entire verse or passage is transcribed.

3. Place the sticky notes in locations that catch your eye frequently throughout the day. Consider high-traffic areas in your home or personal spaces such as your bedroom, bathroom mirror, kitchen sink, or even the laundry room. The objective is to ensure these notes are placed where you're most likely to see them regularly. This method echoes the biblical instruction, "You shall write them on the doorposts of your house and on your gates" (Deut. 6:9), encouraging constant engagement with Scripture.

4. Make a conscious effort to read the Post-it note each time you encounter it. The cumulative effect of these brief, consistent interactions with the text facilitates deep memorization and reflection with minimal disruption to your schedule.

5. To maintain engagement and address any challenges, consider relocating the sticky notes periodically or rewriting them. This refresh can reinvigorate your focus and aid in overcoming any memorization hurdles.

Mirror It

You could also display the verses or passage on your mirror without using sticky notes by using a dry-erase or non-permanent marker to write it directly on the mirror's surface. Doing so ensures consistent exposure to the Word of God and lets you quickly review and read the Scripture whenever you are near the mirror. This simple yet effective technique incorporates the daily routine of using the mirror to deepen your connection with Scripture and internalize it more effectively.

The Glue Method For Memorizing Bible References

How do you memorize the verse locations or references? Have you ever been in a situation where you recall a Bible verse but couldn't remember where it is located in the Bible? By utilizing the glue method, you can ensure that you always know the specific location of a verse whenever you recite it. While it's worth noting that the Bible locations of chapters and verses were not initially included in the Bible, memorizing them can be immensely beneficial for easy reference when needed.

The crucial aspect is to "glue" the verse location to the "END" of the actual verse itself. This method ensures that you memorize the verse location as an integral part of the verse rather than treating it as a separate and distinct element. This method ensures that when the verse is recited, its location naturally follows, making it easy to remember both together.

To further facilitate memorization, I recommend writing out the verse location in words rather than numbers. This approach leverages the brain's tendency to recall words more efficiently than numerical sequences.

For example, instead of writing: **"Your word I have treasured in my heart, that I may not sin against You," Psalm 119:11**, write, **"Your word I have treasured in my heart,**

That I may not sin against You, Psalm one hundred and nine, verse eleven."

This subtle shift in memorization strategy can significantly enhance your ability to recall both the verse and its precise location within the Bible.

SECTION FOUR

15

BENEFIT— LED MORE BY THE HOLY SPIRIT

I will instruct you and teach you in the way which you should go; I will counsel you with My eye upon you.
Psalm 32:8 (NASB 1995)

Your word is a lamp to my feet and a light to my path.
Psalm 119:105

Are you regularly praying for God's guidance in the significant and seemingly minor decisions in your life? Do you deeply desire to discern God's direction for a specific area of your life? The Holy Spirit is indeed ready to guide and unveil the path before you. However, the pivotal question is whether you are receptive to recognizing and adhering to His guidance.

A primary channel through which the Holy Spirit offers direction and timely counsel is the Scriptures. When you have God's Word dwelling in your heart richly, it brings insight and discernment to every new situation. The Holy Spirit can bring relevant Scriptures to your mind that will give you wisdom for the next step you need to take in specific circumstances. However, it's crucial to note that He cannot remind you of Bible Scriptures that you have not already read, spent time contemplating, and memorizing.

Romans 12:2 says, "And do not be conformed to this world, but be transformed by the renewing of your mind, that you may prove what is that good and acceptable and perfect will of God." This means that the deeper we know God's Word and are transformed by it, the better we will discern his specific directions. Since the Bible is our prime source of divine guidance, it is our duty to God to become acquainted and conversant with its contents so that its precepts and principles will become ingrained and implanted in our patterns of thought and action.

If we do not renew our minds daily through the Scripture, we will soon find our minds conformed by default to the temporal value system of this present world that is passing away, and our daily decisions will reflect those values. The more Scripture you hide in your heart, the clearer you will hear the Holy Spirit speak to you. George Müller said, "The Spirit and the Word must be combined. If I look to the Spirit alone without the Word, I lay myself open to great delusions also. If the Holy Ghost guides us at all, He will do it according to the Scriptures and never contrary to them" (n.d.). The Spirit and the Bible work in synergy.

J. C. Ryle was emphatic on this point when he said (2001):

> All who have the Spirit are led by Him to the Scriptures. This is the instrument by which He often works on the soul. The Word is called 'the sword of the Spirit.' Those who are born again are said to be 'born by the Word.' (Eph. 6:17; 1 Peter 1:23.) All Scripture was written under His inspiration —He never teaches anything which is not written there. He makes those in whom He lives to 'delight in the law of the Lord.' (Psalm 1:2.) Just as the infant desires the milk which nature has provided for it, and refuses all other food, so the soul which has the Spirit desires the sincere milk of the Word.

As we search through God's Word, the Spirit opens our eyes to more of what is written there, not just letters and sentences, but a spiritual deposit that speaks to our hearts. As the Bible says in 2 Corinthians 3:6, "For the letter kills, but the Spirit gives life." We need the Holy Spirit as much as we need the Bible; they go hand-in-hand.

Thinking about Scripture throughout your day will help provide you with divine wisdom that will impact every area of your life. It will help you understand God's ways and enable you to apply His principles in your life decisions. By memorizing the Scripture, we are able to have God's wisdom with us at all times. It is written in Luke 2:52 that even Jesus grew in wisdom during his earthly life. Why should we not do the same by memorizing the Word of God, which is the ultimate source of wisdom?

16

STEP 4— MEMORIZE

Keep my commandments and live, And my teaching as the apple of your eye. Bind them on your fingers; Write them on the tablet of your heart.
Proverbs 7:2-3 (NASB)

Even though there are numerous techniques to assist us in memorizing information, the fundamental aspects remain consistent: practice and repetition. The color-coded index cards and other creative strategies still need the tried-and-tested method of layering words upon one another. Much like building a solid foundation, the more slabs of concrete you pour, the thicker and firmer the base will be.

Having prepared your chosen verses or passages as outlined in Step Three—Prepare, it's time to move on to the crucial steps that will help you commit these divine words deeply to memory. Follow these straightforward steps to hide the verses in your heart.

For illustration, let's apply this method to memorize a verse from Isaiah 53 through a series of easy steps:

"Surely he took up our pain

and bore our suffering,

yet we considered him punished by God,

stricken by him, and afflicted" Isaiah Fifty-Three verse Four.

1. **Step One:** Read the first line, "Surely he took up our pain" aloud several times. Each time you read it, emphasize a different word. This technique aids in deepening your understanding of the text, enhancing your focus, and making the learning process both easier and more enjoyable.

For example, start by highlighting "Surely" in your first reading aloud. In your subsequent reading, shift your emphasis to "He." Continue this pattern by then accentuating "took up," followed by a focus on "our," and conclude by emphasizing "pain."

2. **Step Two:** Once you have thoroughly practiced the first step, move on to reciting the line "Surely he took up our pain" from memory. Cover the page or hide the written text, then say the line out loud multiple times. Continue this exercise until you can confidently and accurately recite each word without needing to look at the text.

3. **Step Three:** Next, take line two, "and bore our suffering," and repeat steps one and two until you can recite it faultlessly without relying on the written text. Once you've achieved this, combine lines one and two, reciting them together out loud to ensure accuracy and fluency. Do this several times to prevent the information from fading from your short-term memory. This repetition helps in consolidating your memorization.

4. **Step Four:** Moving on, let's focus on line three, which is "yet we considered him punished by God." Repeat steps one and two above as you did for the other lines until you can say it perfectly. Afterward, challenge yourself to recall lines one, two, and three without referring to the written text. Say them out loud, word-for-word, without any errors. If need be, take a quick look at the written text, just to refresh your memory.

5. **Step Five:** Continue this simple process with each line until you have fully memorized the entire section and can recite it flawlessly. The critical aim here is to achieve error-free recitation. It's vitally important to avoid memorizing a verse incorrectly from the start. Therefore, you should focus on ensuring accuracy in every word, striving for word-for-word precision throughout the memorization process.

How Many Verses Per Day?

If you cannot memorize the entire verse or passage in a single day, don't be discouraged. Simply keep on picking up where you left off, day after day, until you have the verse completely memorized. There is no need to worry about how long it takes to memorize a single verse or even an entire chapter. Remember, the act of hiding God's Word in your heart is not a race; it is a lifelong habit. The ultimate goal is not to become a "Walking Bible" but to develop a deep knowledge of the Lord and to walk closely with Him. So, take your time and focus on the meaningful connection with God rather than rushing through the process.

Indeed, some people can memorize extensive portions of the Bible. Some can even recall the entire contents of up to 20 books of the Bible. Undeniably, this accomplishment is commendable. However, shifting our focus from asking whether we can achieve such feats to asking why we undertake this endeavor is vital. The primary focus should always be how Scripture memorization can help us glorify God and enjoy Him forever.

Word-Perfect

When it comes to memorizing Scripture, the question often arises: is it necessary to memorize verses with absolute precision, or is a close approximation sufficient? The answer is clear: memorizing verses with 100% accuracy and committing them word-for-word to memory is essential.

While some may argue that memorizing approximately 95% of a verse and understanding its general idea is sufficient, especially if slight deviations do not alter the overall meaning significantly, this approach can have drawbacks in the long run. Here's why striving for word-perfect memorization is crucial:

- **Precision in Meaning:** Even minor alterations can significantly impact the interpretation of a verse. The specific choice of words in Scripture is intentional, and each word serves a purpose in conveying the message. A slight change can lead to a misunderstanding of the verse's true meaning.
- **Efficiency in Review:** Experience has shown that memorizing Scripture accurately from the outset makes the review process much smoother and faster. Knowing a verse perfectly means you can recall it with confidence and ease, without second-guessing your accuracy.
- **Confidence in Sharing:** When sharing Scripture with others, whether for encouragement, teaching, or witnessing, confidence in your accuracy is paramount. Knowing that you have memorized the verses correctly allows you to share God's Word with authority and assurance, without the fear of misquoting or misrepresenting the text.

In summary, while getting "close enough" may seem adequate for some, the benefits of word-perfect memorization are clear. It ensures fidelity to the original meaning, facilitates easier review, and bolsters confidence in sharing the Scripture with others. Correctness isn't just key: it's critical. Aim for word-perfect memorization to truly honor and preserve the integrity of the Word of God.

17

PRACTICE—VERBAL

Don't Whisper!

Memorizing Scripture solely in your mind can be challenging and ineffective. With the mind prone to wandering, it's easy to lose focus and drift into unrelated thoughts. Instead of relying on silent repetition, prioritize memorizing and reviewing passages aloud whenever possible. But remember, don't just whisper. Speak clearly and confidently, as if addressing a group or performing on stage.

Imagining yourself as an actor playing a role can also enhance engagement with the text. This practice not only helps maintain focus but also ensures that you're actively listening to how the words sound when spoken aloud. By doing so, you strengthen the process of embedding them into your long-term memory.

Furthermore, this vocalized memorization technique instills confidence that, with the guidance of the Holy Spirit, you can readily recall verses to help others in times of need. So, speak up and let the words resonate, knowing that you're nurturing a deeper connection with Scripture.

Inflect and Accentuate

In addition to reciting verses aloud, inflecting and accentuating your voice can significantly enhance retention by capturing the mood and essence of the text. Experiment with various intonations and pitches to imbue the verses with different emotions and atmospheres, thus deepening your connection to the material.

Try adopting different voices, ranging from deep and authoritative to light and whimsical, or even mimicking sounds like a mouse squeak. Additionally, vary the speed at which you recite the verses, exploring different tempos such as rapid, leisurely, or normal. These variations prevent monotony and fatigue, keeping each repetition fresh and engaging.

By incorporating inflection, accentuation, and tempo variation, you can repeat the verses multiple times without boredom or exhaustion, fostering a dynamic interaction with the text that promotes better understanding and retention.

Pray It

Prayer is another constructive way to write God's Word on the tablet of your heart. From Genesis to Revelation, we discover a wealth of prayers that can enhance and nourish our spiritual lives. Not only can you pray using the prayers of the Bible, but you can also utilize any portion of the Bible to communicate with God in prayer. By personalizing the verses we're memorizing into first-person expressions, we can pray each back to God in worship, confession, thanksgiving, and petition for ourselves and others.

Here's an example of how you can apply this approach using Isaiah 53:5 in prayer:

> Father, I come before You with deep gratitude, acknowledging the sacrifice of Your Son Jesus, whose body was pierced for my transgressions against You. Lord Jesus, I worship You and adore You, for You were crushed for my iniquities. I am profoundly thankful that the punishment that brought me peace with God was placed upon You, and by Your wounds, I am healed. Thank You, Father, for this amazing act of love and grace. In Jesus' name, Amen.

Sing It

Have you ever noticed how much easier it is to remember song lyrics than reciting them without a melody? It's a curious phenomenon why singing helps us retain words more effectively. Perhaps you know the alphabet thanks to the alphabet song or effortlessly recall the major music scale from "Do-Re-Mi" in *The Sound of Music*. Interestingly, many old hymns and worship songs feature lyrics directly drawn from the Bible. It's likely that they were crafted as aids for Scripture memorization.

For thousands of years, people have utilized music as a powerful tool for memorization. So, why not leverage this age-old, powerful tool to internalize the Word of God? Setting Scripture to music not only facilitates quicker memorization but also ensures you retain the information longer.

Now, creating a whole new song might seem daunting, but it's not necessary. You don't need to compose an entire symphony; simply match the words of the verses to a familiar tune. It could be something as basic as "Row, Row, Row Your Boat" or substituting lyrics into a beloved song you already know. The goal isn't to top the charts! Simply use music you already know to aid yourself and others in remembering Bible verses and passages.

Once you've set your Scripture to music, integrate it into your daily routine. Sing it on your commute, while doing chores, during bedtime rituals, or even make it your wake-up alarm or ringtone. A dash of creativity goes a long way.

If you're unsure how to create your own Scripture memory songs, don't fret. There are plenty available online to get you started. Check out resources like:

- *Every Last Word: A Scripture Songs Project* by Matt Papa and Ross King
- *Hide 'Em In Your Heart* by Steve Green. (A great album to learn Bible verses, even if it is aimed at kids.)
- *Scripture Songs for Worship* by Esther Mui.

These resources can jumpstart your journey to memorizing Scripture through song.

18

PRACTICE— AUDIAL

Shadow It

Shadowing is a technique I find particularly effective for memorizing longer passages of the Bible. It not only helps imprint the verses in your heart but also enhances your pronunciation of words, especially the proper names of people and places in Scripture.

Here's how to do it:

1. Get an audio Bible of the version you're memorizing.
2. Take the passage you want to memorize and use an app, such as Audacity, to slow down its tempo. You can find tutorials on YouTube on how to do this effectively.
3. Import the edited audio into your audio player.

4. Listen to the edited audio while simultaneously repeating aloud what you hear, trying to match the narrator's pace and intonation as closely as possible. It's essential to speak at the same time as the narrator, not just repeating after them, although that can also be beneficial. For shadowing or mimicry, aim to repeat simultaneously with the audio Bible.

Shadow Yourself

By using your mobile phone, voice recorder, computer, and so on, you can also record yourself reading the verses aloud and use it for shadowing, as described above.

In addition to actively engaging with the audio version of the Scripture through shadowing, you can further immerse your-self in Scripture passively. Simply play the recordings in the background while you're engaged in routine tasks such as doing laundry, preparing meals, exercising, or commuting.

Listening plays a vital role in the process of memorizing Scripture because it leverages the natural way our memory works. The more we listen to something, the more easily we can remember it. So, why not record the verses or passages you want to memorize and take this with you in the car to play on a continuous loop as you travel or while you are anywhere else you can listen to audio? This repeated listening will allow the Scripture to be deeply embedded in your heart, streamlining the memorization process and ensuring it has a profound and lasting impact.

While Asleep

For those who enjoy having background sounds while sleeping, leveraging audio Bibles could be a unique strategy to deepen your connection with Scripture. Playing these recordings as you sleep may not be the most efficient method for memorizing new and unfamiliar verses, but it could serve as a powerful tool to reinforce the Scripture you've already committed to memory.

19

PRACTICE— SPATIAL

Use It or Lose It!

When memorizing Scripture, it's essential to go beyond mere memorization and focus on valuable application. If you use the passage or verse you are memorizing practically, it reinforces the text in your heart differently than if you only filed that information away in your brain. James 1:22-25 and Joshua 1:8 emphasize that true blessings come from being doers of the Word, not just memorizers.

Therefore, resist the temptation to see learning the text by heart as the goal. Seek to not only understand and memorize the biblical text but much more to take it to heart and apply it. Application is the most crucial step in any successful Scripture memory endeavor. Be sure you live out the text and do not merely memorize it—doing so deceives yourself. After all, the purpose of hiding God's Word in our hearts is to become more obedient to Him as we grow in our knowledge of Him.

It is a common experience that when we actively use a piece of information, it becomes easier to recall. On the other hand, as soon as we stop using that information because it's no longer relevant to our daily lives, it tends to fade away quickly from memory and can eventually be forgotten entirely. To counteract this and ensure the Scriptures you memorize become a living part of your daily life, it's vital to integrate them into your day-to-day activities. Start by thoroughly understanding the text in its context, then move on to pondering its application in your life. You can do this by asking yourself questions aimed at practical application, such as:

- Does this Scripture instruct me with a command I should obey?
- Does it highlight a matter I need to bring before God in prayer, either for myself or as intercession for others?
- Does it highlight an aspect of God's character or work for which I can offer praise and thanksgiving?

Additionally, be watchful and take note of times when the Holy Spirit will bring to your remembrance certain portions of Scripture in a real-life moment of need. If you keep a journal, documenting these instances can be incredibly enriching. It not only serves as a testament to the relevance of God's Word in your life but also strengthens your faith and dependence on divine wisdom for everyday decisions and challenges.

Walk It In

I have observed that memorizing Scripture is much easier for me while walking rather than sitting. I believe this improvement can likely be attributed to the increased oxygenation and blood flow that physical movement promotes, along with the engagement of various muscle groups. These physiological changes help me maintain alertness, engagement, and focus, which are crucial for effective memorization.

Given these benefits, I strongly recommend integrating physical movement into your Scripture memorization routine. Engaging in simple activities such as pacing back and forth in a room, walking along a hallway, using a home treadmill, or even memorizing outdoors in favorable weather conditions can make a significant difference. While sitting or lying down may seem comfortable, these positions may not be as effective for memorization due to the reduced flow of oxygen and nutrients to the brain. However, reciting memorized verses before sleeping can be an exception, as it can aid in reinforcing memory through repetition in a relaxed state.

Move It Out

Adding physical movements to my memorization process has also proven beneficial for retaining scripture. By associating words with body movements, you create muscle memories that can significantly aid in retention. This method leverages the brain's ability to link physical actions with cognitive functions, enhancing the memorization experience.

To employ this technique, think of specific movements that could represent the verses you're memorizing. Get creative and have fun with it—use hand gestures, arm motions, leg movements, head nods, or even full-body actions that correlate with particular words, phrases, or entire verses. The more you physically engage with the material, the more attentive your mind will be. By integrating these movements, you reduce the likelihood of forgetting what you've memorized.

For instance, while memorizing the Sermon on the Mount (Matthew 5-7), I found it helpful to touch my eyes and teeth and even lightly slap my face when reciting Matthew 5:38-39. The verse directly references an "eye for an eye" and "tooth for tooth," along with stating, "If anyone slaps you on the right cheek, turn to them the other cheek, also" (NIV). By connecting these words to my own body, I was able to create a unique and memorable way to link the verses with physical actions, thereby enhancing the memorization process through muscle memory. Challenge yourself to think about how the verse you're studying can relate to your own body or an action you could do!

Give Me a Break!

Starting as a beginner in scripture memorization, you'll gradually find yourself dedicating extended periods to this enriching practice. When you reach this stage, it's important to weave brief, regular breaks into your memorization routine—especially crucial when you begin to notice signs of mental fatigue, reduced focus, or a feeling of disconnection. Pushing through these moments without pausing can hinder your progress, as your brain becomes less adept at processing and retaining the scripture you're working on. Recognizing the moment you start to feel mentally foggy and deciding to take a break is not just advantageous—it's essential for rejuvenating your mental state and ensuring your scripture memorization efforts are fruitful.

During these breaks, engage in activities that relax you without demanding much mental effort. Whether you choose a quiet walk, a refreshing nap, or simply some time with your favorite music, the aim is to relax and allow your brain the opportunity to integrate the scriptures you've recently memorized into your long-term memory. Following such a break, you'll notice an improvement in your mental alertness, which will facilitate a more effective and efficient memorization process. This approach not only enhances your ability to memorize scripture but also ensures that the practice remains a joyful and fulfilling part of your spiritual growth.

The Buddy System

Even if you are diligent, hardworking, and self-motivated, seeking help and support from others can lead to even more significant accomplishments. From my personal experience of learning, one of the most productive ways for me to solidify my knowledge of any topic is to teach it to someone else. With this in mind, I recommend you actively pray and seek opportunities to share what you have memorized with others. Reciting the Scriptures to others, be it your friends, a small group, a class, or during a church service, can be incredibly beneficial.

The intention to share your memory verse or passage after memorizing it can somehow offer an added incentive to ensure thorough memorization, and sharing it will not only edify others but also inspire them to memorize God's Word.

Warning! You may also ask a willing friend, brother, or mere acquaintance who doesn't know the Lord to watch the written text of your memorized passage while you recite it. Ask them to correct you when you make a mistake. Be prepared! You may be surprised by what the Holy Spirit will do with this little way of evangelism.

20

PRACTICE—WRITTEN

CatchWords and CatchPhrases

I have noticed there are parts where I'm bound to make mistakes, and so I'll need a little more effort and skill to deal with them. One of these is verses with a list of words that need to be memorized and recalled correctly in their precise order. For example, Galatians 5:22-23 (NASB) has a list with the words: "love, joy, peace, patience, kindness, goodness, faithfulness, gentleness and self-control." To combat this challenge, I often use what I call a "Catchword & Catchphrase"—or what is popularly called acronyms and acrostics.

These two Scripture memory tools are very common in our ordinary language and are utilized across various fields for their effectiveness in aiding memory. They are so simple that I'm sure pretty much everyone has come across and used them at some point or another. For example, do you remember using ASAP to say "As Soon As Possible"? Do you also recall using the acronym PEMDAS or the acrostic "Please Excuse My Dear Aunt Sally" (or some derivative of this) in math class? You probably do and, as a result, will forever remember the order of operations in mathematics.

Here is how to form an acronym and acrostic:

1. Write the significant words that make up the list in the verse you need to memorize and remember.
2. Underline or highlight only the first letter of each word. This will serve as a trigger or a cue to the actual word or phrase.
3. Form an Acronym: Arrange these initials to create a new, pronounceable word or sequence. It can be nonsensical as long as it's memorable.
4. Create an Acrostic: Sometimes, the underlined first letters may not form a new, easy-to-remember acronym. At such times, using them to form a new sentence, catchphrase, or acrostic may be preferable.

In memorizing Galatians 3:28 with the words: Jew, Gentile, slave, free, male, and female. I made up the acronym JSM, which sounds like GSM.

- J as a cue for "Jew nor Greek"
- S as a cue for "slave nor free"
- M as a cue for "male nor female"

The fruit of the Spirit in Galatians 5:22-23 (NASB) has a list with the words: "love, joy, peace, patience, kindness, goodness, faithfulness, gentleness and self-control." For a beginner, this list of words by itself is tough to remember in the right order, but if you create an acronym or acrostic out of the first letters of each word, they all become much easier to remember.

1. Pick out the first letters of each word: L J P P K G F G S
2. Since creating a straightforward acronym from these first letters proves challenging, the creative and memorable solution will be to make up an acrostic like "Lunatic Justice of Peace Picks King Gong For Governor's Secretary."

These acronyms and acrostics don't need to make much sense; they only need to be memorable, funny, enjoyable, and interesting for you. As long as it tickles you in some way, you're more likely to remember it. Lastly, when you begin to do this, you might find it mentally tiring and too time-consuming to create the acronyms and acrostics, but the more you practice, the more it will become second nature and happen automatically.

Pattern It Out

Since our brains were intricately designed by God to recognize, understand, and remember patterns, we can maximize our memorization efforts tremendously by identifying inherent patterns in our chosen verses or passages. We can practice this with Galatians 5:22-23. Identifying and leveraging the patterns in this passage can profoundly affect how deeply we embed these words in our hearts.

1. Firstly, the passage presents nine character traits representing the fruit of the Spirit, which can be systematically categorized into three groups of three. This 3+3+3 numerical pattern aligns well with our brain's predisposition toward pattern recognition, making it more accessible for us to memorize.

2. Additionally, there's a noticeable progression in syllable count across these three sets, adding another layer of pattern recognition to aid memorization. The first set of traits—love, joy, peace—consists of words with a single syllable each. The second set—pa/tience, kind/ness, good/ness—moves up to two syllables per word. Finally, the third set—faith/ful/ness, gen/tle/ness, and self/con/trol—escalates to three syllables per word.

Rewrite It

Let us apply another famous saying, "Writing once equals reading thrice," to our Scripture memory endeavors. When you've memorized the entire verse or passage and can recite it out loud, challenge yourself by writing it down from memory. Approach this task methodically, transcribing the verse line by line without peeking at your Bible. This experiential application reinforces everything you have memorized and significantly enhances your ability to recall the text, further solidifying the Word of God in your heart.

When you've written it down, take a moment to compare your written version with the actual text in the Bible. Pay close attention to any discrepancies to understand where your memory may have faltered. This step is not merely about identifying errors but is a critical learning moment. It illuminates those parts of the scripture that have not yet been fully committed to memory. By being aware of these gaps, you can direct your efforts toward memorizing and reinforcing those particular sections that require additional practice rather than spending unnecessary time on the parts you already know well.

Embrace Multilingual Approach

This technique may not be suitable for everyone. However, if you are comfortable speaking more than one language, leveraging your multilingual abilities can greatly enhance your scripture memorization efforts.

The technique involves translating the verse or passage you're memorizing into another language. This task demands meticulous attention to detail, compelling you to scrutinize each word closely as you seek out its counterpart in the target language. It's essential to keep the translation as faithful to the original meaning as possible. While striving to maintain the original word order can be helpful, it's understandable that minor adjustments may be necessary to accommodate grammatical differences between languages.

After completing your translation, it's a good practice to compare your rendition with the scripture in a Bible version of the foreign language. This step is crucial for verifying accuracy and understanding.

Engaging in this translation task not only bolsters your memorization, it also deepens your comprehension and connection with the scripture through the lens of different languages.

21

BENEFIT—BE A POWERFUL WITNESS

For I am not ashamed of the gospel, for it is the power of God for salvation to everyone who believes, to the Jew first and also to the Greek.
Romans 1:16

Pray… also for me, that words may be given to me in opening my mouth boldly to proclaim the mystery of the gospel.
Ephesians 6:19

Have you ever shared the gospel with an unbeliever and afterward thought of all the things you wish you had said? This common experience can be minimized by embedding the gospel's truths deep within your heart for timely recollection. What I'm getting at is this: If you have the key verses and passages of the gospel message committed to memory, you'll be prepared to present the gospel using Scripture in those unexpected moments clearly and powerfully. With the help of the Holy Spirit, you will be able to walk the unbeliever through the salvation message, helping them grasp the nature of God: His sovereignty, holiness, justice, goodness, and love, among other aspects. You can also explain the sinful nature of humanity and our desperate need for the Savior, Christ Jesus, who is both fully man and fully God at the same time, in a single person. Additionally, you can delve into the work of the Holy Spirit in terms of regeneration, conversion, repentance, genuine faith, and more.

The role of the Holy Spirit in guiding believers to share the gospel effectively is truly profound. He is uniquely equipped to bring to our minds scriptures we have internalized, especially during those critical moments of evangelism. Such divine prompts enable us to share precisely the right words drawn from Scripture because, as we know, a Christ-exalting text quoted at the right time can be the turning point in a conversation that will result in a non-believer professing faith in the person and work of Jesus Christ.

Sharing Your Personal Testimony vs. the Gospel

However, the question arises: "Is sharing personal testimony sufficient in conveying the salvation message of Christ?" While personal testimonies of transformation are impactful and testify to the power of God in changing lives, they do not, in themselves, constitute the gospel. The gospel is the profound and joyful news of how the triune God—Father, Son, and Holy Spirit—has acted to reconcile and restore fallen, sinful humanity and all of creation back to Himself. This divine plan of redemption was accomplished through the sacrificial work of His Son, the Lord Jesus Christ, and is applied to our lives by the transformative power of His Holy Spirit.

Romans 1:16 emphasizes that it is "the gospel" not "our personal testimonies" that is the power of God unto salvation. If our goal is to see the hearts of others truly changed for the glory of God, we must employ the Scriptures in our evangelistic efforts. Sharing the gospel of Christ instead of your own testimony will give your message divine authority and will harness the penetrating power inherent in the Word of God. Indeed, the Word of God is described in Hebrews 4:12 as "living and active, sharper than any two-edged sword" in its ability to discern the thoughts and intentions of the heart, a quality unique to Scripture alone and not our personal narratives, however valuable they may be.

Romans 10:17 further underscores that faith comes by hearing—not our own testimony, but the Word of God. This is because God's Word informs and convinces the listener of its credibility, reliability, and sufficiency. The Word itself will create in the hearer the faith needed to grasp the gospel message and respond to it.

Therefore, dedicating time and effort to memorizing key Bible verses and passages is not just beneficial but essential for effective evangelism. Armed with the Word of God, you will be better equipped to share the gospel with confidence and clarity, allowing the Holy Spirit to work through you to reach others for Christ. Why not then invest in this eternal endeavor? Why not prepare yourself to be a ready and effective messenger of the gospel to all whom God will bring into your path?

SECTION FIVE

22

STEP 5— HOW TO NEVER FORGET WHAT YOU MEMORIZED

Once you have memorized your selected verse or passage with complete accuracy, the next challenge is how to retain it. How can you avoid forgetting it? How can you keep it fresh in your mind?

Obviously, memorizing Scripture is not like memorizing answers for a test, when you may not care if you remember the information afterward. You don't want just to memorize a verse or passage and then forget it and move on to the next one. You want to retain the Scriptures that you've learned and treasure them in your heart to honor God and receive the blessings of His word continually.

The timeless adage *"repetitio est mater studiorum"* (repetition is the mother of learning) holds a profound truth, especially in the context of scripture memorization. Effective learning and retention demand a regular review of the material already committed to memory. Even a verse memorized to perfection requires periodic engagement to keep it alive in your mind and heart. This principle underscores the importance of consistent reviews to ensure the longevity of memorization.

In any successful Scripture memory program, no principle is more critical than the principle of review. Reviewing is indispensable, as it stands as one of the most enduring methods of learning and is a key to retaining Scripture in your long-term memory. Without sufficient review, the risk of eventually losing a significant portion of what you've memorized increases. The less you revisit and rehearse the Scriptures you've committed to memory, the faster they tend to fade from your recollection. Just as the brain prioritizes the storage of information it deems important, it likewise solidifies and reinforces memories of things encountered frequently and consistently.

Spaced Review

With that said, a common mistake people make is continuously recalling, quoting, or reviewing their memorized verses daily for several weeks, believing it will enhance retention. However, this method often limits the memorization to short-term memory. Conversely, during this review stage, the objective is to transition the memorized Scripture from short-term to long-term memory.

The goal is not to become mere parrots, mindlessly regurgitating Scriptures in fear of forgetting them. Rather, the aim is to retain and retrieve them when needed. This necessitates adapting our approach to ensure that the verses or passages we've learned are stored properly and remain accessible with the help of the Holy Spirit.

Based on my personal experience, I have found that the key to retaining the Scriptures I've memorized for a long time lies in a technique known as "spaced review." This strategy involves gradually increasing the intervals between review sessions. Here's how my spaced repetition schedule looks:

- **Daily Review:** For the first seven days after memorizing a verse or chapter, recite it perfectly once a day.
- **Weekly Review:** Then, dedicate a specific day of the week (e.g., every Monday) to review the verse or chapter aloud once a week for seven weeks.
- **Monthly Review:** Finally, choose a day of the month (e.g., the first of each month) to recite the verse or chapter, continuing this monthly for as long as you find beneficial.

By widening the gaps between each review session, I not only free up mental space and time to memorize new verses, passages, and chapters but also ensure that previously memorized materials are securely locked away in my memory bank.

23

BENEFIT—WORDS SEASONED
WITH SALT

Let your speech always be gracious, seasoned with salt, so that you
may know how you ought to answer each person.
Colossians 4:6

Let no unwholesome word proceed from your mouth, but only such a
word as is good for edification according to the need of the moment, so
that it will give grace to those who hear.
Ephesians 4:29 (NASB 1995)

For Mutual Edification

We cannot live the Christian life alone. God has intentionally built his body, the church, in such a way that each member is dependent upon the other. "The body is a unit, though it is made up of many parts; and though all its parts are many, they form one body. So it is with Christ" (1 Cor. 12:12).

In Colossians 3:16, the Apostle Paul exhorts the believers in Colossae to be ready to teach and admonish one another. However, for this to be possible, we understand from the context that they must let the word of Christ dwell in them richly in all wisdom. The biblical call to love one another, encourage one another, spur one another on, serve one another, instruct one another, honor one another, and be kind and compassionate to one another is impossible unless we are a people rooted and grounded in biblical truth.

So, we must be careful of what is in our hearts and our minds. As Luke 6:45 reminds us, "For out of the abundance of the heart, his mouth speaks." Just as a brimming glass overflows, God's words that fill our minds will spill forth from our lips, uplifting our fellow believers and equipping them for their calling. Our recurrent duty is to support one another on this shared journey, as emphasized in Hebrews 10:24: "And let us consider how to stir up one another to love and good works."

If Scripture is so important to the mutual edification of the body of Christ, it is highly advisable to commit a few key verses and passages to memory. These memorized verses can be invaluable in those moments when we seek to impart guidance and inspiration to others.

Helping Others with Biblical Wisdom

What advice have you offered lately to a family member or a friend? Was this advice based on your own wisdom or the Word of God? If someone were to come to you for advice in a particular situation, would you be able to provide guidance based on biblical principles?

Just as the Holy Spirit retrieves scriptural truth from our memory banks to provide us with timely guidance for our own lives, so He will also bring it to our remembrance for use in counseling others. Knowing Scripture is a vital part of effectively ministering to others.

Committing Scripture to memory will significantly make you far better in sharing with others because you won't merely be expressing personal viewpoints and opinions on the matter, but you will be dispensing the truth of God's Word. With a storehouse of memorized Scriptures, we can readily counsel others by asking, "Would you like to discover what God's Word says about this issue or situation?" In doing so, we can then trust that the Word of God will work effectively in that person's life rather than our own perceived wisdom.

We all desire to assist others in overcoming their issues and challenges, and as a result, we often rush to offer our advice. Nevertheless, regardless of our genuine intentions, our well-intentioned advice can inadvertently misguide those individuals. Communicating God's perspective on a situation will always prove more advantageous than relying only on our well-intentioned counsel. When coupled with the guidance of the Holy Spirit, the Bible never misguides anyone, consistently illuminating the path to clarity in any situation.

As we know, our emotions can get us into trouble, and John MacArthur gives good advice to make sure that we do not fall into the trap of giving emotional advice, "Make more of an effort to read Scripture and memorize important passages. As you saturate your mind with Scripture, you will find your responses are based more on God's truth rather than your emotions" (2022). John Piper sums this up so well as he says, "When the heart full of God's love can draw on the mind full of God's Word, timely blessings flow from the mouth" (2006).

24

IS BIBLE MEMORIZATION ESSENTIAL OR OPTIONAL?

What is the point of memorizing Scriptures when they are readily available to you? This is a valid question, and you may have pondered it, using it as a reason to avoid Bible memorization. If I read the Bible daily as part of my meditation or quiet time with the Lord, wouldn't that be sufficient?

In our present time, we are incredibly fortunate as technology allows us to access any verse we need with just a few taps on our phones. Consequently, there seems to be little necessity to go through the discipline of trying to memorize and recall Bible Scriptures and their references. However, relying solely on this convenience might cause us to miss out on most of the benefits explained in this book.

Matthew Henry presents a compelling argument for why we should not depend solely on having physical Bibles in our hands or digital versions on our phones. He emphasizes the importance of going beyond surface-level engagement and instead allowing the Scriptures to deeply permeate our minds and hearts: "If we have [the Word] only in our houses and hands, enemies may take it from us; if only in our heads, our memories may fail us: but if our hearts be delivered into the mold of it, and the impressions of it remain on our souls, it is safe" (1991).

But more than that, we are commanded to do so.

> *And you must commit yourselves wholeheartedly to these commands that I am giving you today. Repeat them again and again to your children. Talk about them when you are at home and when you are on the road, when you are going to bed and when you are getting up. Tie them to your hands and wear them on your forehead as reminders. Write them on the doorposts of your house and on your gates.* – Deuteronomy 6:6-9 NLT

Some may want to disregard these verses because they are Old Testament. Some might claim that we now operate and live under grace, not under the law to do these things. We do not have to tie little verses around our heads and arms like the orthodox Jews do! But for us today, the passage is a spiritual exhortation to take the Bible so seriously that it is with us when we sleep, wake up, go out, and do our business. The New Testament echoes this sentiment in Colossians 3:16: "Let the word of Christ dwell in you richly."

If anything, we just have to look at examples of godly men who have understood this, taken it to heart, and done it. The account of Jesus in the desert facing temptation and using Scripture is one of the clearest in the Bible. But there are others like Stephen who knew the Scriptures well to be able to quote them so freely in his classic and powerful sermon before the Sanhedrin in Acts 7.

And what more can we say of John Bunyan, who Charles Spurgeon wrote about (1973): "Why, this man is a living Bible! Prick him anywhere—his blood is Bibline; the very essence of the Bible flows from him. He cannot speak without quoting a text, for his very soul is full of the Word of God. I commend his example to you, beloved."

And there is the story about Martin Luther, whose love and grasp of the Bible led him to bring about the Reformation and set the church back on a scriptural foundation. One of the reasons Martin Luther came to his great discovery in the Bible of justification by faith alone was because, in his early years in the Augustinian monastery, he was influenced to love Scripture by Johann Staupitz. Luther devoured the Bible in a day when people earned doctorates in theology without even reading the Bible. Luther said that his fellow professor, Andreas Karlstadt, did not even own a Bible when he earned his doctor of theology degree, nor did he until many years later (Richard Bucher). Luther knew so much of the Bible from memory that when the Lord opened his eyes to see the truth of justification in Romans 1:17, he said, "Thereupon I ran through the Scriptures from memory" in order to confirm what he had found (Piper, 2006).

There are many others, as well! For example, Fanny Crosby, the writer of many of the best-known hymns who spent a significant amount of time memorizing numerous books of the Bible. If they can do it, then there is no excuse for us not to learn a few verses or passages to help our walk with Christ.

25

WHAT TO DO WHEN YOU WANT TO GIVE UP!

For the one who sows to his own flesh will from the flesh reap corruption, but the one who sows to the Spirit will from the Spirit reap eternal life. And let us not grow weary of doing good, for in due season we will reap, if we do not give up.
Galatians 6:8-9

Therefore, my beloved brothers, be steadfast, immovable, always abounding in the work of the Lord, knowing that in the Lord your labor is not in vain.
1 Corinthians 15:58

Whether we are trying to learn a second language, prepare for ministry, write a book, obtain a college degree, raise godly children, build a startup company, or stick to a healthier diet, many of life's most meaningful goals require a great deal of perseverance. Perseverance is the dominant ingredient in every success story. There are many inspiring true stories of average men and women throughout history who have accomplished fantastic and impressive things. With persistence, they were able to achieve stunning victories against seemingly insurmountable odds. For example, think of how Noah persevered and built the Ark over the course of 50-75 years, being surrounded by wicked and corrupt unbelievers. While passion and planning are great, perseverance is the critical element that will get you to the finish line every time.

Though it is true that it is God who is at work in us both to will and to do that which brings glory to His name, it is also true that every mature Christian you will ever meet knows one thing by experience: That without the ability to truly persevere, they simply would not have made it to where they are today. Without determination, steady persistence, tenacity, and patience in their walk with God, especially in spite of difficulties or discouragement, they simply would not have achieved the spiritual growth they desired. And without such perseverance, neither can you.

What I mean is that, in reality, Scripture memorization in the long run usually comes down to one thing: the art of perseverance with the help of the Holy Spirit. So, whether you're aiming to memorize entire books of the Bible or wanting to reach a smaller goal of treasuring short verses in your heart, you're going to need to know how to persevere. Why? Because there will inevitably be times when things just don't seem to be going your way, times when things don't go as planned, and life just happens.

So, what do you do when the going gets tough and when your energy is flagging? What do you do when you're so down or stressed that giving up on Scripture memory seems the best option? Stay diligent! Persevere and don't give up! Though you may feel like taking the easy way out, which is usually quitting, if you keep at it, you'll eventually find fulfillment just as the river finds the ocean at the end. The rewards of knowing God experientially and of growing in intimacy with Him will make your labor worthwhile in the face of these challenges. The ride is going to be worth it if you keep persevering.

Now here are three tips to ensure that you press on, even when the going gets tough:

Pray!

Memorizing Scripture, if used for the glory of God, launches you into a spiritual battle. Satan will stop at nothing to hinder you from learning Bible verses to keep you from growing in your intimacy with Jesus. So, the first thing to do when you feel like giving up, is to cry out to God your Father in prayer! Tell him exactly how you feel. Ask Him to help you and strengthen you with power through His Spirit in your inner being. He has promised to uphold you with His righteous right hand. Remember it's Him who works in you, both to "will and do" memorizing Scripture, for His name, glory, and good pleasure. So cry out to your Father! (Isa. 41:10; Phil. 2:13; Eph. 3:16)

Your Big Whys

Getting clear about your **"Big Whys"** is an excellent strategy for perseverance. So, every now and then, remind yourself why you're doing this. What's the purpose of memorizing Scripture? What would it lead to? What would hiding God's Word in your heart do in you and for you?

Your **"Big Whys"** may include some of the benefits explained in this book. For example:

- Are you really hungry to know God more deeply?
- How much do you desire to be transformed and conformed into Christ's likeness?
- Do you yearn to be continually led and guided by the Holy Spirit?
- Do you want your prayers to avail much and receive answers?
- Would you like to experience more daily triumphs over temptation, sin, Satan, and the flesh?
- Would you like to become a more effective soul winner, witnessing with confidence for the Lord Jesus?

I would also recommend that you boldly write out your *big whys* and place them where you'll see them every day to keep your spirits high, maintain enthusiasm, and be in charge of your emotions!

Reach Out

Thirdly, reach out and call a brother or sister in the Lord, or even your pastor for encouragement. Let someone encourage you and hold you accountable to continue the race you are running. As you keep putting one foot in front of the other, I promise that one day you will look back and see that you've climbed a mountain of memorizing an entire verse, chapter, or book of the Bible.

I plead with you: Don't give up! Don't give in! Don't stop trying! And if you give in to any challenge for a short moment, pray, get up, brush yourself, and pick up where you left off. But don't ever, ever give up!

My beloved brothers and sisters, the rewards are priceless! God has many blessings for you that will be discovered ONLY when you persist in hiding his word in your heart. And now you have at your fingertips five easy-to-use practical steps, lots of tried and true ideas, and tools to hopefully keep you traveling in this lifelong journey of treasuring the Scriptures in your heart!

FINAL REQUEST

Dear Friend,

If you've found value in this book and believe its message is worth sharing, please leave an honest review on platforms like Amazon, Apple Books, Google Books, Kobo, Audible, or wherever you accessed this book. The impact of reviews on a potential reader's decision cannot be overstated; both the number of reviews and the overall rating are critical factors that prospective readers consider when determining a book's appeal and relevance. Your thoughtful review could serve as a pivotal encouragement for others to delve into this book, potentially leading them to a deeper, more impactful walk with Christ through the memorization of the Word of God. I'm grateful for your willingness to share your insights and help extend the book's reach. Thank you for your valuable contribution to this ongoing spiritual conversation.

REFERENCES

Alcorn, R. (2010, August 18). *Charles Spurgeon on knowing Christ - resources.* Eternal Perspective Ministries. https://www.epm.org/resources/2010/Aug/18/charles-spurgeon-knowing-christ/

Andrei, M. (2021, March 9). *That "Memory Palace" thing? It actually works, a new study finds.* ZME Science. https://www.zmescience.com/medicine/mind-and-brain/memory-palace/

Bonhoeffer, D., & Riess, J. (2012). *God is in the manger: Reflections on Advent and Christmas.* Westminster John Knox Press.

Broadbent, K. (2021, April 7). *4 different learning styles: The VARK theory.* Melioeducation.com. https://www.melioeducation.com/blog/vark-different-learning-styles

Brody, B. (2022, August 23). *Why can't I remember anything?* WebMD. https://www.webmd.com/balance/guide/why-cant-i-remember

Brooks, T. (2013). *The privy key to heaven.* Bottom of the Hill Publishing.

Brooks, T. (2018). *Precious remedies against Satan's devices.* Charles Rivers Editors.

Chambers, O. (2000). *My utmost for His highest.* Barbour & Co.

desiringGod. (2017, February 6). *How do I pray the Bible?* Desiring God. https://www.desiringgod.org/interviews/how-do-i-pray-the-Bible

ElearningWorld Admin. (2017, October 23). *Quote of the week.* Elearning-World. https://www.elearningworld.org/quote-of-the-week-14/

English standard version Bible. (2001). Crossway Bibles.

Flavin, B. (2019, May 6). *Different types of learners: What college students should know.* Rasmussen University. https://www.rasmussen.edu/student-experience/college-life/most-common-types-of-learners/

Gallaty, R. (2017, February 2). *The importance of Scripture memory.* CSB. https://csBible.com/search/talmud/

GeorgeMuller.org. (n.d.). *George Muller quotes.* GeorgeMuller.org. https://www.georgemuller.org/quotes

Grace Gems. (n.d.). *Short pithy gems from JC Ryle.* Grace Gems. https://www.gracegems.org/30/short_pithy_gems_from_jc_ryle.htm

Gurnall, W. (2010). *The Christian in complete armour.* Hendrickson Publishing Group.

Guthrie, G. H. (2011). *Read the Bible for life: Your guide to understanding & living God's word.* B & H Pub.

Halloran, K. (2015, May 22). *Charles Spurgeon's 9 tips for Christian readers (quotes on books) anchored in Christ.* Kevin Halloran. https://www.kevinhalloran.net/charles-spurgeons-9-tips-for-christian-readers/

Harvard Health. (2020, March 30). *7 ways to keep your memory sharp at any age.* Harvard Health. https://www.health.harvard.edu/healthbeat/7-ways-to-keep-your-memory-sharp-at-any-age

Harvard University. (2011). *How memory works.* Derek Bok Center for Teaching and Learning. https://bokcenter.harvard.edu/how-memory-works

Henry, M. (1991). *Matthew Henry's commentary on the whole Bible: Complete and unabridged.* Hendrickson Publishing Group.

Holy Bible, KJV. (2014) Thomas Nelson Pub.

Holy Bible: New living translation. (2015). Tyndale House Publishers.

Klett, L. M. (2019, June 11). *Chinese Christians memorize Bible in prison: Gov't "can't take what's hidden in your heart."* The Christian Post. https://www.christianpost.com/news/chinese-christians-memorize-Bible-prison-cant-take-whats-hidden-in-your-heart.html

Luther, M., & Leupold, U. S. (1965). *Liturgy and hymns.* Fortress Press.

MacArthur, J. (2011). *Evangelism: How to share the gospel faithfully.* Thomas Nelson.

Moody, D. L. (2019). *Anecdotes and illustrations of D.L. Moody: Related by him in his Rrvival work.* Forgotten Books.

Müller, G. (2017). *Answers to prayer.* Bridge-Logos Publishers.

Murray, A. (2018). *Like Christ: Thoughts on the blessed life on conformity to the Son of God.* F.H. Revell.

New American standard Bible. (1998). Foundation Publications.

NIV study Bible. (2011). Zondervan Pub. House.

Packer, J. I. (1999). *Knowing Christianity.* Intervarsity Press.

Piper, J. (2006, September 5). *Why Memorize Scripture?* Desiring God. https://www.desiringgod.org/articles/why-memorize-Scripture

Platt, D. (2010). *Radical: Taking back your faith from the American Dream.* Multnomah.

PreceptAustin. (2022, January 30). *Memorizing His Word.* Precept Austin. https://www.preceptaustin.org/memorizing_his_word

Riddle, D. R. (2007). *Brain aging: Models, methods, and mechanisms.* Taylor & Francis.

Ryle, J. C. (2001). *Having the Spirit.* Inheritance Publishers.

Ryle, J. C. (2018). *Expository thoughts on the gospels.* Hansebooks GmbH.

Ryle, J. C. (2021). *How do you read the Bible?* The Banner of Truth Trust.

Selderhuis, H. J. (2017). *Martin Luther: A spiritual biography.* Crossway.

Sherman, J. (2020, February 2). *Bible Memory for eternal impact.* UFC Women. https://ufcwomen.blog/2020/02/02/Bible-memory-for-eternal-impact/

Sletten, D. R. (n.d.). *A perspective on our mental processes versus our physical brain.* Access Research Network. http://www.arn.org/docs/sletten/Mind-Brain-Processes-Rev-D.pdf

Sproul, R. C. (2006). *A taste of heaven: Worship in the light of eternity.* Reformation Trust Pub.

Sproul, R. C. (2009). *The prayer of the Lord.* Reformation Trust Pub.

Sproul, R. C. (2017, December 1). *What Is the Mind?* Tabletalk. https://tabletalkmagazine.com/article/2017/12/what-is-the-mind/

Spurgeon, C. H. (1973). *Autobiography* (Vol 2). Banner Of Truth Trust.

Spurgeon, C. H. (2013). *The complete works of Spurgeon* (Vol. 29). Delmarva Publications.

Spurgeon, C. H. (2016). *Morning and evening.* Discovery House.

Torrey, R. A. (2020). *Person and work of the Holy Spirit.* Digireads Com.

UNC. (2018). *Memorization Strategies.* Learning Center. https://learningcenter.unc.edu/tips-and-tools/enhancing-your-memory/

Washer, Paul. (2012). *Christ, the True Vine* [Video]. YouTube. https://www.youtube.com/watch?v=2T44BhY2d74

Watson, T. (2012). *A Christian on the mount: A treatise concerning meditation.* Bottom of the Hill Publishers.

Webb, L. (2018, September 1). *Renewing your mind.* Tabletalk. https://tabletalkmagazine.com/article/2018/09/renewing-your-mind/

Wesley, J. (2012). *The works of the Rev. John Wesley* (Vol. 5). Ulan Press.